GOODSON MUMBA

Organizational Behavior

Insights and Strategies

Copyright © 2024 by Goodson Mumba

All rights reserved. No part of this publication may be reproduced, stored or transmitted in any form or by any means, electronic, mechanical, photocopying, recording, scanning, or otherwise without written permission from the publisher. It is illegal to copy this book, post it to a website, or distribute it by any other means without permission.

First edition

ISBN: 9798335229364

This book was professionally typeset on Reedsy. Find out more at reedsy.com

Contents

Preface		iv
Acknowledgement		vi
Dedication		vii
Disclaimer		viii
1	Chapter 1: Understanding Organizational Behavior	1
2	Chapter 2: Personality and Attitudes	18
3	Chapter 3: Motivation at Work	38
4	Chapter 4: Communication in Organizations	60
5	Chapter 5: Group Dynamics and Teamwork	83
6	Chapter 6: Leadership in Organizations	106
7	Chapter 7: Decision Making	126
8	Chapter 8: Power and Politics in Organizations	145
9	Chapter 9: Conflict and Negotiation	168
10	Chapter 10: Organizational Culture	192
11	Chapter 11: Change Management	216
12	Chapter 12: Technology and Innovation	239
13	Chapter 13: Ethics and Corporate Social Responsibility	263
14	Chapter 14: Work-Life Balance	287
15	Chapter 15: Looking Ahead: The Future of Organizational...	307
About the Author		331

Preface

Welcome to "Organizational Behavior: Insights and Strategies." This book aims to explore the intricate dynamics of human behavior within organizational settings, providing a comprehensive understanding of how individuals and groups interact within professional environments. The importance of this subject cannot be overstated, as the success of any organization largely depends on the effective management of its most valuable resource: its people.

Organizational behavior is a multidisciplinary field that draws from psychology, sociology, anthropology, and management. It seeks to understand and predict human behavior in an organizational context, offering strategies to foster a positive work environment, enhance productivity, and achieve organizational goals. In today's rapidly changing business landscape, the ability to navigate the complexities of human behavior is more crucial than ever.

The purpose of this book is twofold. First, it aims to provide students, academics, and practitioners with a solid foundation in the theories and principles of organizational behavior. By delving into key topics such as motivation, leadership, team dynamics, and organizational culture, readers will gain valuable insights into the factors that influence behavior at work. Second, this book offers practical strategies and tools that can be applied to real-world situations, bridging the gap between theory and practice.

Throughout the chapters, you will find a blend of classic theories and contemporary research, reflecting the evolving nature of the field. Case studies, real-world examples, and interactive exercises are incorporated to enhance understanding and engagement. Each chapter concludes with a set of discussion questions and activities designed to encourage critical thinking and application of the concepts covered.

This book is the result of collaborative efforts from experts in the field of organizational behavior. We extend our gratitude to the contributors, reviewers, and everyone who played a role in bringing this project to fruition. Their diverse perspectives and expertise have enriched the content and ensured that it addresses the needs of a wide audience.

We hope that "Organizational Behavior: Insights and Strategies" will serve as a valuable resource for those seeking to understand and improve human behavior in organizations. Whether you are a student embarking on a journey into the world of organizational behavior, a manager looking to enhance your leadership skills, or a scholar conducting research, we trust that you will find this book both informative and inspiring.

Thank you for choosing this book. We invite you to explore its pages with curiosity and an open mind, and to apply its lessons in your professional endeavors.

Sincerely,

Goodson Mumba

Acknowledgement

I would like to eternally and gratefully acknowledge the Almighty God for the infinite intelligence from His universal mind where we draw from all that we come to know and are yet to know. May I also acknowledge and thank everyone that has played a part in my journey of life in terms of spiritual, moral, emotional and material support.

Dedication

I extend my sincerest gratitude to my beloved wife, Edith Mumba, and our children, Angelina, Lubuto, Letticia, Lulumbi, and Butusho, for their unwavering support and understanding throughout the conception, writing, and eventual publication of this book, despite the sacrifices and challenges they endured.

Disclaimer

This book is a work of fiction. Names, characters, businesses, places, events, and incidents are either the products of the author's imagination or used in a fictitious manner. Any resemblance to actual persons, living or dead, or actual events is purely coincidental.

1

Chapter 1: Understanding Organizational Behavior

It's a brisk Monday morning at OptiTech's sleek headquarters in Silicon Valley. The open floor plan buzzes with the ambient clacking of keyboards and murmured conversations, as employees prepare for the week's pivotal launch. The air is electric—charged with anticipation and a hint of underlying tension.

Characters:

- **Elena Myles:** The CEO of OptiTech, whose vision for the future of technology is unmatched, but whose leadership style often feels erratic to her team.
- **Jack:** The experienced Marketing Head, loyal but increasingly frustrated with the chaotic direction of the company.
- **Aisha:** A young, brilliant programmer known for her assertiveness and innovative ideas that often push the boundaries of the company's norms.

- **Lin:** The CFO, whose calm demeanor is being tested by the company's financial risks and creative disorder.

Dramatic

Elena's Challenge: In the gleaming glass office overlooking the bustling floor, Elena stands contemplating the sprawling digital maps and code on the screens. Her mind races with possibilities and fear—fear that her inability to harness the collective potential of her team could lead to failure. The product launch looms large, and the stakes couldn't be higher.

Jack's Dilemma: Below, Jack arranges his notes for the marketing strategy, his expression one of concern. He's seen many product launches, but none with so much internal discord. He wonders how to align his campaign with a product that even the developers seem unsure about, given the last-minute changes Elena often pushes for.

Aisha's Frustration: Across the room, Aisha types furiously, her brow furrowed. She's coding complex algorithms, but her mind is also racing with questions about the company's future and her role in it. She feels stifled by the lack of clear direction and longs for the opportunity to really showcase her capabilities.

Lin's Anxiety: In a quieter corner, Lin reviews financial projections, her lips pursed. The numbers don't look good. The investment in the AI project has drained resources, and the return is anything but guaranteed. She needs to prepare to advise Elena on possible cutbacks, knowing well how her suggestions might be dismissed.

The Meeting: The tension culminates at the weekly team meeting where Elena, enthusiastic yet visibly stressed, presents her vision for the launch, expecting excitement but meeting skepticism. Jack raises concerns about market readiness, Aisha questions the product's evolving features, and Lin cautiously hints at budget overruns.

As voices rise, Elena realizes she must bridge the gap between her visionary ideals and her team's operational realities. This chapter delves into the essence of organizational behavior—the interplay of individual actions, team dynamics, and leadership styles that shapes the success or failure of an organization.

Through OptiTech's story, this chapter explores foundational theories of organizational behavior, showing how understanding personality traits, communication flows, and leadership effectiveness can turn turmoil into triumph. It sets the stage for a deeper exploration into specific strategies that could help Elena and her team not just survive but thrive.

Elena ends the meeting with a decision to seek help. She plans a corporate retreat focused on team-building and strategic alignment, hoping it can mend the fractures and align their efforts. As everyone leaves the room, there's a shared sense of cautious optimism. Maybe, just maybe, understanding each other's behaviors and motivations is the first step toward a unified path forward.

Definition and Scope of Organizational Behavior

The day after the heated team meeting, Elena arranges a follow-up session specifically designed to address the fundamentals of organizational behavior. She hopes that by bringing everyone onto the same page about the science behind their interactions, the team can reset their dynamics towards a more productive and harmonious working environment.

Elena opens the session in the conference room, where the sunlight softly illuminates the array of skeptical but curious faces of her team. With a deep breath, she begins to explain the core of what they need to address, turning the discussion towards the very foundation of their workplace dynamics.

Elena's Explanation: Elena told the team that organizational behavior is essentially the study of how people interact within groups. Its main purpose is to apply such knowledge to improve an organization's effectiveness. She emphasized that it's a bridge between human behavior and the organization itself, and understanding it can lead to better decision-making and planning.

Jack's Interjection: Jack noted that this means considering everything from individual employee attitudes and personality traits to the broader systems in place which guide how they all work together. He suggested that by applying organizational behavior theories, they could identify where miscommunications are most likely to occur and why certain initiatives might be met with resistance.

Aisha's Insight: Aisha chimed in, reflecting on how understanding organizational behavior could help them better manage the change that comes with their constant innovations. She said that knowing how people respond to change can guide how they introduce new technologies or workflows to the team.

Lin's Contribution: Lin spoke about the scope of organizational behavior extending beyond just office interactions. She mentioned its implications for everything from recruitment to training, leadership development, and even customer relations. Understanding it, she pointed out, could help them better align their financial strategies with human resources.

Group Discussion: The team then engaged in a group discussion about how each of their roles intersects with the principles of organizational behavior. Elena listened as they explored how their daily tasks and challenges could be viewed through this lens, leading to a shared realization about the potential for improved communication and team cohesion.

Elena's Closing Remarks: Elena concluded the session by reiterating that the purpose of diving deep into organizational behavior was not just academic but a practical necessity. She stated that by understanding and implementing its principles, they could enhance not only their working relationships but also the overall performance and success of OptiTech.

The team left the meeting with a new appreciation for the complexities of their interactions and a stronger grasp of how intentional adjustments in behavior could drive better outcomes. There was a renewed sense of commitment to applying these insights, starting with the upcoming retreat Elena had planned.

As the team dispersed, there was a palpable shift in the atmosphere. Knowledge had replaced confusion, strategy had taken the place of chaos, and a pathway to realignment seemed not just necessary, but achievable. Elena watched her team leave, feeling more hopeful about their collective future than she had in months.

Historical Development of the Field

In an effort to deepen the team's understanding and commitment to applying organizational behavior principles, Elena schedules a series of brief educational sessions. Each session is crafted to bridge historical insights with their current challenges. The first of these sessions takes place in a relaxed setting within the company's library, surrounded by books and artifacts that represent decades of industry innovation.

Elena, with the help of a guest speaker, Dr. Liam Chen, a renowned expert in organizational behavior, prepares to take the team on a journey through the history of the field. As everyone settles around the antique oak conference table, the air fills with a mix of curiosity and the faint scent of old paper.

Elena's Introduction: Elena introduced Dr. Chen, highlighting his expertise and his role in shaping contemporary organizational behavior strategies. She explained that understanding the historical context would help them see the relevance of these theories in today's tech-driven world.

Dr. Chen's Presentation: Dr. Chen began his talk by tracing the roots of organizational behavior back to the early 20th century with the advent of Taylorism, or scientific management, which emphasized efficiency and productivity through the analysis of workflows and behaviors. He noted that this was the first major framework to consider workers in terms of behavioral components at work.

Transition to Human Relations Movement: Dr. Chen described how the Hawthorne Studies in the late 1920s and early 1930s revolutionized the field by highlighting the psychological aspects of work, such as employee morale and leadership styles. This marked a pivotal shift from viewing workers merely as cogs in a machine to recognizing their emotional and social needs at work.

The Rise of Modern Theories: Moving through the timeline, Dr. Chen touched upon the rise of various organizational behavior theories in the 1960s and 1970s, such as Douglas McGregor's Theory X and Theory Y, which posited that management style was heavily influenced by the manager's perceptions of worker motivations.

Relating to OptiTech's Culture: As Dr. Chen discussed the evolution of theories focusing on workplace diversity, culture, and technology's role in organizational behavior, Jack and Aisha exchanged looks of realization. The historical context began to frame their current challenges in a new light, particularly around how they could manage their diverse team more effectively.

Interactive Discussion: The session became interactive, with team members asking Dr. Chen how historical shifts might mirror some of the digital and cultural transformations their company was experiencing. Lin queried about the impact of remote work trends on organizational dynamics, a particularly relevant topic given the company's increasing flexibility.

Elena wrapped up the session by thanking Dr. Chen and reflecting on the importance of learning from the past to manage the future. She emphasized that the evolution of organizational behavior is much like the evolution of technology—they are both responses to new challenges and new opportunities.

As the team left the library, there was a shared sense of enlightenment about how their work connected to a larger historical narrative. Elena sensed a growing enthusiasm among the team, not just to apply these lessons to their current project, but to be part of the ongoing evolution of organizational behavior themselves. This historical perspective had provided them with a broader understanding of their place within the tapestry of workplace dynamics, empowering them to shape the future of OptiTech with renewed vigor and insight.

Key Concepts and Theories

Following the historical overview provided by Dr. Chen, Elena arranges a workshop aimed at deep diving into the key concepts and theories of organizational behavior that are particularly relevant to OptiTech's environment. The setting is the company's main collaboration space, transformed into a learning hub with whiteboards filled with diagrams and sticky notes highlighting various theories.

The atmosphere is charged with a collaborative spirit as Elena, alongside a behavioral consultant, Maya, prepares to guide the team through the core theories that underpin effective organizational behavior. Their goal is to not only educate but also to facilitate direct application of these concepts to OptiTech's ongoing projects and challenges.

Elena's Opening Remarks: Elena began the session by emphasizing the importance of understanding these foundational theories as tools that could help decode and influence their everyday interactions and decision-making processes. She introduced Maya, who would help illustrate these concepts with interactive exercises.

Maya's Introduction to Key Theories: Maya started with an overview of **Maslow's Hierarchy of Needs**, using it to explain how individual employee motivations could vary widely depending on their personal and professional stages in life. She mapped this theory to their project teams, suggesting ways to better motivate employees by understanding their specific needs.

Interactive Activity on McGregor's Theory X and Theory Y: Maya then shifted to McGregor's theories, setting up role-play scenarios where Jack and Aisha acted out management styles that treated team members under assumptions of Theory X (people dislike work) versus Theory Y (work can be as natural as play if conditions are favorable). This helped the team visualize the impact of leadership perceptions on employee performance and morale.

Group Discussion on Herzberg's Two-Factor Theory: Next, Maya facilitated a group discussion on Herzberg's Motivation-Hygiene Theory, asking the team to list factors that led to satisfaction and dissatisfaction in their current roles. Lin, drawing from her own experiences, pointed out how policy and administration changes had a significant impact on team morale and productivity, resonating with Herzberg's emphasis on hygiene factors.

Application of Social Learning Theory: Maya introduced Bandura's Social Learning Theory by highlighting the role of observational learning in the workplace. She used recent project debriefs as examples, showing how employees learn behaviors from one another. This segment concluded with strategies to foster positive role modeling and reduce negative mimicking within teams.

Relevance of Equity Theory: The session concluded with an exploration of Adams' Equity Theory, where Maya explained how perceptions of unfairness could demotivate employees. She engaged the team in a candid conversation about perceived inequities at OptiTech and brainstormed ways to address these issues constructively.

Elena closed the session by reflecting on how these theories could be directly applied to enhance leadership strategies, improve communication, and boost employee engagement. She stressed the importance of ongoing education and adaptation of these theories to keep up with the changing dynamics of their team and industry.

As the workshop ended, the team felt a newfound clarity and empowerment. Theories that once seemed abstract were now tangible tools that could be wielded to sculpt a healthier, more productive workplace culture. With these insights, they were ready to tackle their project hurdles with innovative approaches, feeling more connected as a cohesive unit ready to face the technological frontiers ahead.

The Role of Organizational Behavior in Management

Motivated by the previous sessions' revelations, Elena decides to cap the week with a crucial seminar focused on the specific applications of organizational behavior in management. The venue is OptiTech's main auditorium, now arranged to foster a roundtable discussion among leaders and team members alike. At the center of the stage is a large screen, ready to display insights and frameworks.

The auditorium buzzes with anticipation as the team gathers, notebooks at the ready, to uncover how organizational behavior principles can directly influence and enhance management practices at OptiTech. Elena, with her renewed focus, aims to bridge the gap between theoretical understanding and practical application, ensuring her management style and that of her team leaders are both inspired and informed by solid behavioral insights.

Elena opened the seminar by outlining her vision for a management approach that is deeply informed by the principles of organizational behavior. She emphasized the need for leaders at OptiTech to not only manage projects and deadlines but to also manage the human elements of their teams.

Interactive Panel Discussion: Elena introduced a panel of experts in organizational behavior and management, including Maya, the behavioral consultant. The panel was tasked with discussing key areas where organizational behavior impacts management, such as leadership development, conflict resolution, and employee motivation.

Keynote on Leadership and Organizational Behavior: Maya delivered a keynote on the transformational leadership model, discussing how it leverages understanding of human behavior to inspire and engage employees. She detailed how leaders like Elena could use empathy and clear communication to foster a positive environment that drives innovation and commitment.

Real-Life Case Studies: The discussion shifted to real-life case studies presented by Jack and Lin. Jack shared a recent challenge where team motivation dipped and how he applied motivational theories to turn the situation around. Lin discussed her approach to handling financial stress within teams, utilizing organizational behavior insights to ensure her messages were clear and supportive rather than punitive.

Workshop on Conflict Resolution: A workshop followed, led by a guest expert in industrial-organizational psychology.

The focus was on practical strategies for conflict resolution, emphasizing the need for understanding individual behaviors and triggers in conflict situations. Participants role-played scenarios based on recent tensions within OptiTech, applying techniques discussed to de-escalate conflicts effectively.

Elena concluded the seminar with a passionate talk about the integral role that understanding organizational behavior plays in effective management. She pledged to incorporate these insights into her daily management practices and encouraged her team leaders to do the same.

As the seminar came to a close, the team reflected on the profound impact that a deeper understanding of organizational behavior could have on their roles as managers and leaders. They recognized that managing well means more than just overseeing tasks; it means nurturing a team's spirit, aligning individual goals with company objectives, and creating an environment where innovation thrives.

Leaving the auditorium, there was a palpable sense of empowerment among the OptiTech team. They had begun to see themselves not just as managers, engineers, or marketers, but as stewards of a living, breathing organizational culture poised for success. Elena watched her team disperse, her heart buoyed by the thought that they were not just ready to face the challenges ahead but equipped to transform them into opportunities for growth and excellence.

Interdisciplinary Influences

After the enlightening seminar on management and organizational behavior, Elena schedules a creative session to explore the interdisciplinary influences on organizational behavior.

She arranges for this meeting in OptiTech's innovation lab, a space filled with gadgets and screens that reflect the fusion of multiple disciplines. It's a relaxed environment with lounge areas and interactive digital displays, intended to stimulate creative thinking.

As the sun sets casting long shadows across the lab, team members from diverse departments gather, bringing with them perspectives shaped by their varied academic and professional backgrounds. Elena, energized by the previous discussions, is eager to demonstrate how disciplines such as psychology, sociology, anthropology, and even engineering intersect with organizational behavior to create a rich tapestry that can enhance management and operational strategies at OptiTech.

Elena's Introductory Talk: Elena opened the session by expressing her fascination with how different fields contribute unique insights into organizational behavior. She introduced guest speakers from each discipline to illustrate these intersections and their practical applications in a tech environment.

Guest Speaker on Psychology: The first speaker, a psychologist, explained how psychological principles apply to understanding individual differences and dynamics within teams. She discussed cognitive biases, perception processes, and personality traits that influence employee behavior and decision-making.

Sociology Presentation: A sociologist took the stage to discuss the role of social structures and cultural influences within the workplace. He emphasized how social norms and group dynamics can affect communication and collaboration, presenting case studies from global companies to illustrate his points.

Anthropology Insights: An anthropologist shared her insights into how cultural backgrounds influence workplace values and ethics. She explained the concept of cultural relativism and its impact on how organizational policies are perceived and implemented by employees from different cultural backgrounds.

Engineering Perspective: An engineer from OptiTech discussed how technological tools and interfaces could be designed to enhance organizational behavior strategies, focusing on user experience (UX) design principles that facilitate better communication and workflow efficiencies.

Interactive Panel Discussion: After the presentations, Elena facilitated a panel discussion where team members could ask questions and explore how these interdisciplinary approaches could be integrated into their current projects. Jack questioned the practical application of psychological theories in marketing strategies, while Aisha explored how cultural insights could influence her software development work.

Elena closed the session by emphasizing the importance of embracing these interdisciplinary insights to foster a holistic understanding of organizational behavior at OptiTech. She encouraged her team to consider these diverse perspectives not only in their professional roles but also in how they interact with each other daily.

The team left the session with a deeper appreciation for the complexity of their work environment and the multiple layers of human interaction it entailed. They felt more equipped to approach their projects with a broader, more inclusive viewpoint, considering not just the technical requirements but also the human element in everything they do.

As the lights dimmed in the innovation lab, the members of OptiTech felt a renewed sense of purpose. They were not just employees in a tech company but participants in a dynamic field that intersected with myriad disciplines, each providing essential keys to understanding and improving the workplace. Elena watched with pride as conversations continued around her, the seeds of interdisciplinary appreciation already sprouting promising ideas for the future.

Current Trends and Future Directions

Building on the momentum from the interdisciplinary session, Elena decides to hold a forward-thinking workshop focusing on the current trends and future directions in organizational behavior. The venue is OptiTech's high-tech conference room, redesigned for an immersive experience with virtual reality (VR) stations and augmented reality (AR) displays, symbolizing the cutting-edge future they're navigating.

It's a crisp, clear morning, and as the team gathers, the energy is palpable. They're not just meeting to discuss future trends; they're about to experience them. Elena, with her innate sense for dramatic flair, has set up the room to not only talk about the future but to step into it, using technology to highlight how these emerging trends could directly impact their work at OptiTech.

Elena's Visionary Opening: Elena opens the session with a vibrant keynote on how the understanding and application of organizational behavior must evolve as rapidly as technology does. She emphasizes the need to stay ahead of behavioral trends that are shaped by advancements in AI, remote work technologies, and global collaboration tools.

Showcase on AI and Machine Learning: A tech expert from OptiTech demonstrates how AI and machine learning can analyze employee data to predict trends, enhance employee engagement, and personalize the work experience. The demonstration includes a live simulation showing AI suggestions for team restructuring based on communication patterns and project outcomes.

Discussion on Remote Work and Flexibility: The team moves to a VR setup where they experience a virtual OptiTech office, designed to support a fully remote workforce. Here, Elena discusses the trend towards increased workplace flexibility and its implications for organizational behavior, focusing on maintaining culture and cohesion without physical presence.

Interactive AR Presentation on Global Teams: Using augmented reality, a consultant shows how virtual teams across different continents can interact in real-time, highlighting the importance of understanding cross-cultural organizational behavior to foster effective global collaboration.

Panel on Sustainability and Organizational Behavior: A panel featuring young leaders from within OptiTech speaks about integrating sustainability into the core of business operations and how it influences organizational behavior, driving a shift towards more ethical and environmentally conscious decision-making.

Elena's Futuristic Close: Elena concludes the workshop by reflecting on how these trends necessitate a new approach to managing and leading. She calls on her team to be pioneers, not just in technology, but in how they embody the principles of organizational behavior to create a resilient, adaptive, and

CHAPTER 1: UNDERSTANDING ORGANIZATIONAL BEHAVIOR

inclusive workplace.

As the session ends, team members are buzzing with ideas and discussions about how these trends could be implemented into their current projects and daily operations. There's a sense of excitement about the possibilities that lie ahead, with a clearer understanding of how their roles need to evolve to meet the future head-on.

Leaving the conference room, the OptiTech team feels more connected than ever to the future trajectory of their industry. They are not just passive observers of change but active participants shaping the future of work. Elena watches her team, inspired by their enthusiasm and commitment, knowing that together, they are ready to turn these insights into actionable strategies that will propel OptiTech into a new era.

2

Chapter 2: Personality and Attitudes

After a groundbreaking session exploring the current trends and future directions in organizational behavior, Elena pivots to a new chapter in her efforts to strengthen OptiTech's team dynamics. This time, the focus is on the individual elements at play within the team—the varied personalities and attitudes of her employees. Elena decides to hold a day-long workshop in OptiTech's airy, sunlit atrium, transforming the space into a series of interactive personality assessment stations, mood boards, and open dialogue circles.

The day is devoted to uncovering and understanding the complex tapestry of personalities and attitudes that influence the workplace environment at OptiTech. Elena, aware of the sensitivity of the topic, begins with a personal story about her journey in understanding her own leadership style and how it has been shaped by her personality traits and attitudes towards work. Elena stands before her diverse team, sharing insights from her personal reflections and professional feedback over the years. She emphasizes the value of self-awareness in personal and professional growth and introduces the team to the tools they'll be using throughout the day, including the Big Five personality test and the Attitudes Toward Work survey.

Interactive Personality Assessment: The team splits into smaller groups, rotating between stations where they complete various personality assessments. Facilitators guide them through the process, ensuring everyone understands the purpose and how these insights can be applied in their roles.

Debriefing Session on Big Five Outcomes: After the assessments, the team regroups for a facilitated debriefing session led by a psychologist specializing in workplace behavior. The psychologist presents aggregated results from the Big Five personality test, highlighting the diversity of personalities within the team and discussing how these traits can influence work behavior, team cohesion, and conflict resolution.

Attitudes Toward Work Discussion: Elena leads a session discussing the Attitudes Toward Work survey results, focusing on how employee satisfaction, commitment, and work involvement affect their daily productivity and overall company culture. She opens the floor for employees to share their feelings and experiences, facilitating a transparent dialogue about what motivates and frustrates them.

Role-Playing Exercises: In the afternoon, the workshop shifts to role-playing exercises where team members enact scenarios based on typical workplace conflicts and challenges. Each role-play incorporates different personality types and attitudes to illustrate how these elements can clash or harmonize, providing practical examples of how to manage diverse behaviors effectively.

As the sun begins to set, casting long shadows across the atrium, Elena gathers her team for a closing circle. She reflects on the day's activities and the revelations they've shared. Elena stresses the importance of empathy and tailored communication, encouraging her team to consider personality and attitude nuances when interacting with each other.

The team leaves the workshop with a deeper understanding of themselves and their colleagues. The atmosphere is one of renewed respect and empathy, as team members appreciate the unique contributions and perspectives each person brings to OptiTech.

Elena watches her team disperse, feeling a mixture of pride and optimism. She knows that the insights gained today about personality and attitudes are just the beginning of a more harmonious and dynamic work environment. This understanding lays the groundwork for more effective teamwork and leadership, essential for navigating the challenges and opportunities that lie ahead for OptiTech.

Personality Traits and Workplace Performance

After a morning filled with personality assessments and insightful discussions, Elena decides to steer the workshop towards a more focused analysis of how specific personality traits directly influence workplace performance. OptiTech's collaborative workspace is rearranged into a series of breakout areas, each themed around one of the Big Five personality traits: Openness, Conscientiousness, Extraversion, Agreeableness, and Neuroticism. Each area is equipped with case studies, real-life examples from within OptiTech, and guided activities designed to illustrate the impact of these traits on work behavior.

Elena, acting both as facilitator and participant, moves between the stations, engaging with her team and observing the dynamics as they explore the deeper implications of personality traits on their daily work lives.

Elena's Guided Tour through the Traits: Elena begins the segment by explaining how each personality trait can influence aspects of workplace performance. She uses an interactive digital board to display data from various studies linking personality traits with job performance, adaptation to change, leadership effectiveness, and team dynamics.

Openness Station: At the Openness station, Elena presents examples of how team members high in this trait have successfully spearheaded innovative projects at OptiTech. She discusses how their willingness to explore unconventional solutions and embrace new technologies has led to breakthroughs in product development. The group engages in a brainstorming activity, applying openness to problem-solving scenarios.

Conscientiousness Workshop: Moving to the Conscientiousness area, Elena highlights how this trait correlates with reliability and attention to detail—key factors in OptiTech's quality assurance processes. Team members share personal stories where high conscientiousness has helped them meet tight deadlines and manage complex projects effectively.

Extraversion Discussion Circle: In the circle of Extraversion, Elena focuses on the energizing effect of extroverted employees in team settings and customer interactions. A role-play exercise demonstrates how extraverts improve team morale and client relations, but also how they need to balance their approach to include introverted team members.

Agreeableness Conflict Resolution Role-Play: At the Agreeableness station, the group tackles the trait's role in facilitating team harmony and collaborative success. Through conflict resolution role-play, participants see how agreeableness can lead to positive negotiations but might also limit assertiveness in critical decision-making situations.

Neuroticism and Stress Management Workshop: Finally, at the Neuroticism station, Elena addresses how higher levels of this trait can impact stress management and decision-making under pressure. The session includes stress-reduction techniques and discussions on how to support colleagues who may experience higher levels of workplace anxiety.

As the workshops conclude, Elena brings everyone together for a final reflection. She emphasizes the importance of balancing and harnessing different personality traits to optimize performance and achieve a supportive, productive workplace environment.

The team leaves the session with a profound understanding of how intrinsic personality traits affect their interactions and contributions at work. They feel equipped with strategies to leverage their strengths and address challenges, enhancing personal and team performance.

Elena watches as her team discusses their next steps, animated with new insights and mutual understanding. She feels a sense of accomplishment; not only has she deepened her team's knowledge of themselves and each other, but she has also planted the seeds for a more adaptive and resilient OptiTech. This day marks a significant step towards aligning personal growth with organizational success.

The Big Five Personality Model

After exploring how individual personality traits impact workplace performance, Elena decides to delve deeper into the Big Five Personality Model, setting the stage for a more structured exploration. She organizes a series of workshops held in OptiTech's main conference room, now creatively divided into five distinct zones, each representing one of the Big Five traits: Openness, Conscientiousness, Extraversion, Agreeableness, and Neuroticism. Each area is visually distinct, reflecting the essence of the trait it represents with colors, images, and interactive displays.

As the team members enter the room, they're handed personalized maps that guide them through the zones, encouraging them to engage with activities and discussions tailored to each trait. Elena opens the session with an overview of the Big Five model, explaining its relevance in personal development and team dynamics.

Standing at the center of the room, Elena addresses her team with a mix of enthusiasm and seriousness. She explains that the Big Five model is a tool for understanding human behavior more scientifically, and mastering it can lead to better self-awareness and more effective interpersonal interactions.

Workshop Activities in Each Zone:

1. **Openness Zone:**

   - This area features abstract art and innovative tech demos.

Team members engage in brainstorming sessions that challenge them to think outside the box, reflecting the trait of openness to experience.
- Elena circulates, observing and occasionally participating in discussions about how openness influences adaptability and creativity in tech development.

1. **Conscientiousness Zone:**

- Decorated like a high-efficiency workspace, this zone emphasizes order and attention to detail. Activities include game-like challenges that require careful planning and precision.
- Elena uses this zone to highlight the value of conscientiousness in achieving high-quality results and maintaining reliable work processes.

1. **Extraversion Zone:**

- This brightly lit area with upbeat music features networking exercises and team presentations. It's vibrant and social, designed to bring out the lively interactions typical of extraverts.
- Elena points out how extraversion contributes to building strong networks and effective communication within the team.

1. **Agreeableness Zone:**

- A cozy, comfortable space with a roundtable for facilitated discussions on conflict resolution and collaborative

tasks.
- Here, Elena discusses the importance of agreeableness in fostering a cooperative team environment and how it can be balanced with assertiveness to avoid conformity and passivity.

1. **Neuroticism Zone:**

- This area offers a calm oasis with resources on stress management and emotional regulation workshops. It aims to address the challenges associated with high neuroticism.
- Elena spends time here explaining strategies for resilience and stability in high-pressure situations, reassuring her team about the support available.

Elena's Conclusive Talk: As the workshops wind down, Elena gathers everyone back at the center of the room. She reflects on the insights gained and the importance of understanding these personality dimensions. She emphasizes how leveraging this model can enhance team synergy and individual career paths within OptiTech.

The team leaves the session with a deeper appreciation of how diverse personality traits shape their workplace. They feel more equipped to leverage their strengths and address their weaknesses, contributing to a more dynamic and harmonious work environment.

Elena watches as her team disperses, chatting animatedly about their experiences in each zone. She feels a sense of satisfaction knowing that today's exercise has not only brought them closer together but also made them more introspective and understanding of their diverse personalities. This, she believes, is the foundation of a truly innovative team, ready to tackle the challenges and opportunities ahead with renewed vigor and mutual respect.

Attitude Towards Work; Commitment, Satisfaction, and Involvement

After exploring the Big Five personality traits, Elena turns her attention to attitudes towards work. She recognizes that understanding commitment, satisfaction, and involvement is crucial for fostering a positive workplace culture. Elena converts a section of OptiTech's spacious lounge into a "Reflection Room," designed with comfortable seating areas, motivational posters, and feedback stations equipped with interactive digital surveys and personal reflection journals.

The Reflection Room buzzes with a soft, contemplative energy as the team gathers. Soft lighting and gentle background music set a reflective mood. Elena, keen to connect on a deeper level with her team's work attitudes, introduces the day's focus with a brief but passionate talk about the importance of aligning personal values with their work.

Elena's Introductory Remarks: Elena opens with a personal anecdote about her own career journey, discussing moments of high commitment and satisfaction, as well as times of doubt. She explains that understanding these attitudes can lead to more meaningful work and a more cohesive team environment.

Interactive Stations:

1. **Commitment Station:**

- At this station, team members are invited to participate in activities that measure their emotional, continuous, and normative commitment to the company. They use apps to navigate scenarios where their commitment levels are tested and provide feedback on what drives their loyalty and tenure at OptiTech.
- Elena circulates, engaging in discussions about what commitment looks like in day-to-day operations and how it can be fostered through leadership and policy.

1. **Satisfaction Station:**

- Here, employees fill out anonymous digital surveys that assess job satisfaction facets such as work-life balance, recognition, and job security. Results are displayed in real-time on screens, showing a heat map of satisfaction levels across different departments.
- Elena uses this data to initiate small group discussions, exploring how job satisfaction impacts productivity and well-being, and what steps can be taken to enhance it.

1. **Involvement Station:**

- This space focuses on measuring how deeply employees feel involved in their work and the company's mission. It features interactive case studies where employees can suggest improvements or new ideas for projects,

reflecting their level of psychological involvement and personal investment.
- Elena listens intently to the suggestions, noting how involvement can lead to better innovation and engagement, discussing strategies to increase this sense across all teams.

Group Discussions: Elena gathers everyone for a facilitated discussion about the interconnections between commitment, satisfaction, and involvement. She leads a brainstorming session on potential initiatives that could improve all three dimensions, such as flexible working hours, enhanced recognition programs, and more inclusive decision-making processes.

As the session concludes, Elena reflects on the insights gained and the shared experiences of the team. She emphasizes that their attitudes towards work are not static and can be shaped by conscious efforts from both management and employees. She commits to taking the feedback seriously and working on actionable plans to address the areas of concern.

The team leaves the Reflection Room feeling heard and valued. They appreciate the opportunity to express their views and are encouraged by Elena's commitment to making tangible changes based on their input.

As the lights dim in the Reflection Room, Elena feels a profound connection with her team. She knows that fostering positive attitudes towards work is an ongoing journey, one that requires empathy, flexibility, and commitment. With the insights from today's activities, she is more confident than ever that OptiTech can become a place where everyone feels committed, satisfied, and deeply involved in their work.

Personality Assessments and Their Use in HR Practices

After successfully diving deep into the attitudes towards work, Elena turns her focus to integrating personality assessments into OptiTech's human resources practices. She organizes a strategic workshop in the company's training room, now configured as a high-tech seminar space with multiple screens displaying various assessment tools and real-time data analysis software. The setting is professional yet inviting, designed to encourage open discussions about the practical applications of these tools.

As team members file into the room, they're greeted by stations set up to demonstrate different personality assessments, including the Myers-Briggs Type Indicator, the DISC Assessment, and newer AI-driven tools. Elena, alongside OptiTech's HR director, Lucas, prepares to show how these tools can be used not just for recruitment, but for ongoing development and team building.

Elena's Opening Presentation: Elena begins the workshop with a clear vision: to enhance hiring practices, personalize employee development programs, and improve team dynamics using data-driven insights from personality assessments. She stresses the importance of ethical considerations and the responsible use of such tools to avoid pigeonholing or bias.

Live Demonstration:

- **Recruitment Simulation:**
- Lucas conducts a live simulation of a candidate evaluation, showing how personality assessments can complement traditional interviews. The simulation reveals how

these tools help predict candidate success in various roles and cultural fit within teams.
- Elena discusses the implications of these insights, emphasizing the goal of creating diverse and complementary teams rather than homogeneous groups.
- **Development Program Customization:**
- The next station showcases how HR can use assessment results to tailor professional development plans that align with individual employees' personality traits and career aspirations.
- Elena engages with the team to brainstorm personalized training programs, such as leadership tracks for high conscientiousness employees or creative problem-solving workshops for those high in openness.

Interactive Session on Team Building:

- Elena and Lucas facilitate an interactive session where they use assessment results to assemble project teams for a hypothetical new initiative. Participants use the data to debate and decide team compositions, considering factors like balancing different personality types to maximize cohesion and productivity.
- This exercise highlights the practical benefits and challenges of applying personality assessments in real-world team settings.

Panel Discussion on Ethics and Privacy:

- A panel featuring an organizational psychologist and a data privacy expert is convened to discuss the ethical implications of using personality assessments in the workplace.
- The discussion covers consent, transparency, data handling, and the importance of using assessment outcomes constructively and non-discriminatorily. Elena ensures that these values are understood as foundational to their HR practices.

Elena's Conclusive Remarks: As the workshop concludes, Elena reiterates her commitment to using these tools responsibly to enhance OptiTech's workplace culture and operational efficiency. She announces the creation of a new task force, led by Lucas, to oversee the integration of personality assessments into various HR functions, ensuring ongoing evaluation and adaptation of these practices.

The team leaves the workshop with a nuanced understanding of how personality assessments can be a powerful tool in shaping a dynamic and supportive workplace. They appreciate Elena's balanced approach to innovation in HR practices, respecting individual differences while striving to optimize team performance.

Elena watches as her team discusses their own experiences and ideas sparked by the day's activities. She is confident that these efforts to weave scientific tools into the fabric of OptiTech's culture will lead to a more engaged, productive, and satisfied workforce, ready to meet the challenges of the future with resilience and creativity.

The Impact of Personality and Attitudes on Team Dynamics

Following the enlightening workshop on personality assessments, Elena organizes a session dedicated to exploring the practical implications of personality traits and attitudes on team dynamics. She chooses OptiTech's newly designed collaboration space, a vibrant area equipped with modular furniture and digital screens for interactive simulations and real-time feedback.

The collaboration space is alive with anticipation as team members gather, intrigued by the promise of gaining deeper insights into how their unique personalities and attitudes shape their interactions and collective output. Elena, keen to build on the momentum of the recent sessions, has prepared a series of activities and discussions designed to illuminate the complex interplay between individual characteristics and team effectiveness.

Elena's Introductory Overview: Elena starts the session with an overview of the day's goals, explaining that understanding the impact of personality and attitudes on team dynamics is crucial for achieving synergy and avoiding conflict. She highlights that today's exercises will help everyone better understand their role within the team, fostering a more cohesive and supportive work environment.

Activity 1: Personality Role Mapping:

- Elena directs the team to a station where they are asked to map out their personality traits using the Big Five model and discuss how these traits might influence their role in

a team setting.
- Each member shares their profile, providing personal anecdotes about times when their traits have positively or negatively affected team outcomes. This exercise fosters empathy and deeper understanding among teammates.

Activity 2: Attitude Alignment Workshop:

- The next activity focuses on attitudes towards work—commitment, satisfaction, and involvement. Team members fill out a quick survey, and results are projected in real-time, showing a spectrum of attitudes present within the team.
- Elena facilitates a discussion on how these varying attitudes can impact team morale and productivity. She encourages the team to brainstorm strategies to align their attitudes more closely, such as setting shared goals or celebrating team successes together.

Simulation: Conflict Resolution Scenarios:

- Using interactive software, Elena sets up simulated workplace scenarios that involve conflicts arising from clashing personalities or differing attitudes.
- Team members role-play different solutions, using techniques discussed earlier in the day. This hands-on approach helps them visualize the direct effects of their personality and attitudes on team dynamics and learn constructive conflict resolution methods.

Panel Discussion: Integrating Insights into Daily Work:

- Elena invites a panel of senior team leaders and a behavioral psychologist to discuss ways to integrate the day's insights into everyday work practices at OptiTech.
- They cover topics such as adapting leadership styles to suit team personality compositions and creating feedback mechanisms that respect individual attitudes while promoting team unity.

Elena's Conclusive Reflection: As the day draws to a close, Elena gathers the team for a final reflection. She expresses her gratitude for their openness and engagement throughout the activities and emphasizes the importance of continuing to apply these insights moving forward.

The team leaves the session with a renewed sense of understanding and appreciation for the diversity within their ranks. They recognize how their individual traits and attitudes contribute to the team's overall dynamic and are more equipped to leverage these for collective success.

Elena watches as her team disperses, chatting animatedly about the insights they've gained. She feels a profound sense of achievement, knowing that today's exercises have not only strengthened the team's interpersonal relationships but also equipped them with the tools to thrive in a complex, ever-changing work environment.

Adapting Leadership Styles to Personality Types

Encouraged by the success of the previous sessions, Elena organizes a focused case study workshop to explore how leadership styles can be adapted to different personality types within OptiTech. The setting is OptiTech's main auditorium, transformed into a collaborative learning environment with multiple round tables, each equipped with tablets loaded with interactive case studies and personality assessment tools.

As the team members settle into their seats, they find a personalized folder at each table containing details of their personality profiles and a summary of leadership theories. Elena, determined to drive home the practical applications of the theories discussed, prepares to guide her team through a series of case studies that highlight the effectiveness of adaptive leadership.

Elena's Introduction to the Workshop: Elena opens the session with an energetic welcome, briefly recounting the journey they've embarked on to understand the nuances of personality and leadership. She sets the stage for the day's goals: to identify which leadership styles best align with various personality types and how shifting one's leadership approach can dramatically improve team dynamics and performance.

Interactive Case Study Breakdown:

- **Case Study Introduction:**
- Elena presents the first case study, featuring a tech startup where the CEO struggled to manage a diverse team, leading to high turnover and low morale. The CEO's

leadership style is described, and team members are asked to assess the personality types of both the leader and the team members involved.
- **Group Analysis:**
- Team members break into small groups to discuss the case. They use tablets to explore different leadership styles (transformational, transactional, situational) and analyze which might have been more effective given the team's personality composition.
- Each group uses a digital whiteboard to map out their findings, considering factors such as the need for stability, creativity, structure, and empathy.

Role-Playing Exercise:

- After discussing the first case, Elena transitions the workshop into a role-playing exercise. Participants assume the roles of various leaders and team members from the case study, experimenting with different leadership styles.
- This hands-on activity helps team members feel the impact of leadership decisions tailored to personality types, illustrating how changes in approach can lead to better engagement and outcomes.

Expert Panel Discussion:

- Elena invites a panel of leadership development experts to provide feedback on the groups' analyses and role-playing outcomes. The experts discuss the merits and challenges of adapting leadership styles to suit team personality dynamics, offering additional insights from psychological and managerial perspectives.

- As the workshop concludes, Elena gathers the team for a closing reflection. She emphasizes the importance of flexibility and awareness in leadership, highlighting how an adaptable leader can foster a positive and productive work environment.
- She encourages her team to consider their own leadership approaches or how they are led, and to seek continual growth in aligning their methods with the needs of their colleagues.

The team leaves the session equipped with a deeper understanding of how effective leadership is not a one-size-fits-all approach but a dynamic interplay between leader and team personalities. They appreciate the tangible examples provided, which offer clear strategies for application in their roles.

As the team exits the auditorium, discussions abound about applying the day's lessons to their daily interactions and leadership roles within OptiTech. Elena watches with pride, confident that the insights gained today will not only enhance leadership effectiveness but also elevate OptiTech's entire organizational culture.

3

Chapter 3: Motivation at Work

After successful sessions on personality and leadership adaptation, Elena decides it's time to tackle a new challenge: motivation at work. Understanding that motivation is a cornerstone of productivity and satisfaction, she organizes a day-long retreat at a scenic lakeside venue just outside the city, aiming to combine a serene environment with deep discussion and introspective activities. The retreat includes motivational workshops, guest speakers, and interactive team-building exercises.

The morning air is crisp and refreshing as the OptiTech team arrives at the lakeside retreat. The natural beauty of the surroundings and the informal setting provide a perfect backdrop for unwinding and opening up to new learning experiences. Elena greets her team with enthusiasm, eager to explore the intricacies of workplace motivation.

Elena begins the retreat with an inspiring speech about the power of motivation and its profound impact on both individual and collective success. She introduces the day's agenda, which includes exploring different motivational theories, identifying personal and team motivators, and developing strategies to enhance workplace motivation.

Workshop on Motivation Theories:

- **Theory Overview:**
- The first workshop delves into classic and contemporary motivation theories, such as Maslow's Hierarchy of Needs, Herzberg's Two-Factor Theory, and Deci and Ryan's Self-Determination Theory. Each theory is presented through engaging multimedia presentations.
- **Group Discussion:**
- Teams discuss how these theories apply to their experiences at OptiTech. They share personal stories where certain needs, whether for esteem, achievement, or relatedness, significantly influenced their work output and satisfaction.

Guest Speaker Session:

- Elena invites a renowned psychologist specializing in industrial-organizational behavior to talk about the latest research in motivation. The speaker discusses intrinsic versus extrinsic motivation and introduces cutting-edge findings on gamification and its effectiveness in the workplace.
- The talk concludes with practical tips on how managers can create an environment that fosters intrinsic motivation, emphasizing autonomy, mastery, and purpose.

Team-Building Exercise:

- Post-lunch, Elena leads a team-building exercise where small groups tackle a series of challenges that require cooperation, creativity, and problem-solving. Each activity is designed to help team members understand the role of support and recognition in enhancing motivation.
- Teams must identify what motivates their members during the activity and use this to strategize their approach to challenges.

Development of Personal Motivation Plans:

- In the late afternoon, Elena facilitates a workshop where each team member creates a personal motivation plan. This plan includes setting short and long-term goals, identifying needed resources, and outlining steps to increase their own intrinsic motivation at work.

As the sun sets over the lake, Elena gathers everyone for a closing circle. She emphasizes the importance of continuing to cultivate an environment where motivation thrives through understanding, support, and appropriate challenges.

The team leaves the retreat feeling rejuvenated and motivated. They have a clearer understanding of what drives them individually and as a team, and they are equipped with practical tools to enhance their motivation.

As they board the bus back to the city, conversations buzz with plans and ideas for applying the day's insights. Elena looks on, satisfied with the day's outcomes, knowing that a motivated team is the engine that will drive OptiTech's growth and innovation.

Overview of Motivation Theories (Maslow, Herzberg, McGregor)

To further the understanding of motivation within OptiTech, Elena organizes an immersive, educational workshop held in the company's main conference room, now converted into thematic areas representing each motivational theory. The room is designed to facilitate interaction and reflection, with visual aids, quotes, and interactive digital displays about Maslow's Hierarchy of Needs, Herzberg's Two-Factor Theory, and McGregor's Theory X and Y.

As OptiTech's team members enter the conference room, they are greeted by distinct stations, each vividly illustrating the core concepts of the three seminal motivation theories. Elena, with her characteristic enthusiasm, welcomes everyone and explains how these theories apply not just in abstract but in their everyday work scenarios.

Elena's Introductory Presentation: Elena starts with a brief introduction, outlining the significance of understanding various motivational theories to better manage and inspire their diverse team. She emphasizes that while these theories were developed in different eras, the essence of what they teach about human motivation remains relevant today.

Interactive Station Activities:

1. **Maslow's Hierarchy of Needs:**

- **Visual Journey:**

- Team members walk through a large, pyramid-shaped installation, with each level representing a different need: physiological, safety, love/belonging, esteem, and self-actualization. Interactive prompts ask participants to reflect on and record which level they feel they're currently at in their professional lives.
- **Group Discussion:**
- At the top of the pyramid, a facilitated discussion encourages team members to share how their needs affect their motivation and performance at work, fostering a deeper personal connection to Maslow's theory.

1. **Herzberg's Two-Factor Theory:**

- **Dual-Sided Room Setup:**
- The room is split into two areas: 'Hygiene factors' and 'Motivators'. Each side has descriptions and examples of factors such as company policy, salary, interpersonal relations (hygiene), and achievement, recognition, the work itself (motivators).
- **Interactive Voting:**
- Employees use digital kiosks to vote on which factors they find most motivating or demotivating, with real-time results displayed on monitors. This visual feedback sparks a conversation on improving workplace conditions and job satisfaction.

1. **McGregor's Theory X and Y:**

- **Role-Playing Scenarios:**
- This station features role-playing activities where par-

ticipants assume managerial roles under Theory X (assuming employees are inherently disinterested in work) and Theory Y (believing employees are self-motivated). Each scenario plays out common workplace situations, illustrating the impact of managerial assumptions on employee motivation.
- **Reflective Debrief:**
- Following the role-plays, a debrief session helps participants reflect on the effects of leadership styles influenced by McGregor's assumptions, discussing which style might be more effective in various OptiTech teams.

After rotating through the stations, Elena gathers the team for a wrap-up discussion. She highlights key takeaways and asks the team to consider how these theories might influence their approach to projects and interactions at OptiTech. She encourages everyone to think about ways to apply these insights to enhance motivation within their teams.

As the workshop concludes, team members express a newfound appreciation for the complexity of motivation and its critical role in their work environment. They leave with specific ideas on how to apply these theories to increase job satisfaction and productivity within their teams.

Elena watches her team depart, energized and thoughtful. She is confident that the deeper understanding of motivation gained today will lead to more effective leadership and a more fulfilling work environment at OptiTech, ultimately driving the company's success.

Application of Motivation Theories in the Workplace

With OptiTech's team now well-versed in the foundational theories of motivation, Elena decides it's time to put theory into practice. She transforms OptiTech's innovation lab into a series of real-world simulation environments where teams can apply the motivational concepts they've learned. Each simulation is crafted to reflect typical scenarios at OptiTech, ranging from meeting project deadlines under stress to innovating new product ideas.

As the team members enter the revamped innovation lab, they find it divided into zones that each represent a different department within OptiTech—R&D, Marketing, HR, and Operations. Each zone challenges teams to apply specific motivational theories to solve problems or enhance productivity. Elena, overseeing the operations with a keen eye, encourages everyone to think creatively and leverage their new knowledge to enhance their work experiences.

Elena's Introductory Brief: Elena opens the session with a brief reminder of the theories covered—Maslow's hierarchy, Herzberg's two-factor theory, and McGregor's Theory X and Y—and explains how each theory can be strategically applied in different workplace contexts. She sets the stage for a day of active learning, emphasizing that today's experiences are designed to make these theories tangible and directly applicable.

Simulation Activities:

1. **R&D Zone - Applying Maslow's Hierarchy of Needs:**

- **Scenario:**
- Team members are presented with a scenario where they need to innovate under tight deadlines. The simulation includes variables that affect physiological needs (comfortable workspaces), safety needs (job security), and self-actualization (opportunities for creative expression).
- **Application:**
- Teams are tasked with arranging their work environment and schedule to meet these needs, enhancing their collective creativity and satisfaction.

1. **Marketing Zone - Herzberg's Two-Factor Theory:**

- **Scenario:**
- The marketing team faces a campaign that failed to meet expectations. They need to analyze hygiene factors (like salary and work conditions) and motivators (like recognition and achievement) to propose improvements.
- **Application:**
- Participants use digital tools to redesign job roles and develop new recognition programs that enhance job satisfaction and drive better campaign results.

1. **HR Zone - McGregor's Theory X and Y:**

- **Scenario:**
- HR managers need to address high employee turnover

rates. They assess current management styles and their impacts on employee motivation and retention.
- **Application:**
- Through role-playing, team members explore and debate the effectiveness of Theory X versus Theory Y management styles, aiming to adopt a more motivational and trusting approach in their policies.

1. **Operations Zone - Self-Determination Theory (Deci and Ryan):**

- **Scenario:**
- Operations staff struggle with autonomy and procedure-heavy tasks that lower their intrinsic motivation.
- **Application:**
- Teams redesign workflows to increase autonomy, competence, and relatedness among staff, applying self-determination principles to increase motivation and productivity.

After the simulations, Elena gathers everyone for a debriefing session. She facilitates a discussion on the lessons learned, challenges faced, and the practical benefits of applying motivational theories in their everyday tasks. She encourages her team to think of ways these theories can be continuously integrated into their daily routines at OptiTech.

The team leaves the session energized and equipped with practical strategies to enhance their motivation and that of their colleagues. The hands-on application of motivational theories not only brings new insights but also reinforces the team's ability to innovate and adapt these concepts to their specific roles within OptiTech.

As the lab doors close behind the last of the departing team members, Elena reflects on the day's successes. She is confident that the active application of motivational theories has prepared her team to tackle their projects with renewed vigor and understanding, setting the stage for a more motivated and productive workplace at OptiTech.

Goal-Setting and Its Impact on Employee Performance

After a series of successful simulations demonstrating motivational theories in practice, Elena recognizes the need to focus on goal-setting—a critical component that directly impacts employee performance and motivation. She organizes a dynamic workshop in OptiTech's main assembly hall, now arranged with visual goal-setting stations, interactive displays, and tools for personal and team goal formulation.

As the OptiTech team gathers in the transformed assembly hall, they are greeted by an atmosphere charged with the potential for personal and professional growth. Each station is designed to help them visualize and articulate their goals, from immediate project targets to long-term career aspirations. Elena, enthusiastic about the transformative power of effective goal-setting, kicks off the event with a motivational speech.

Elena's Motivational Opening: Elena opens the workshop with an inspiring talk on the significance of setting clear, achievable goals. She explains how goal-setting not only enhances performance but also boosts motivation by providing a clear roadmap for success. She introduces the concept of SMART goals (Specific, Measurable, Achievable,

Relevant, Time-bound) and challenges everyone to apply this framework during the workshop.

Interactive Goal-Setting Activities:

1. **Personal Goal-Setting Station:**

- **Activity:**
- Team members use digital tablets to draft their personal SMART goals, focusing on both short-term objectives and long-term career plans. Facilitators roam the room, offering guidance and feedback.
- **Impact:**
- Participants reflect on their professional paths and identify precise steps to advance their skills and contributions at OptiTech.

1. **Team Goal Formulation Area:**

- **Activity:**
- In this collaborative space, each departmental team works together to set collective goals that align with OptiTech's strategic objectives. This includes project deadlines, innovation targets, and team-building outcomes.
- **Impact:**
- Teams discuss and align their aspirations, enhancing unity and shared commitment to the group's success.

1. **Visualization Corner:**

- **Activity:**

- Here, employees create visual representations of their goals using boards, markers, and digital design tools. This creative expression helps solidify their intentions and makes the goals more tangible.
- **Impact:**
- Visualizing goals helps to embed them more deeply in the participants' minds, making them more impactful and easier to recall.

1. **Progress Tracking Tools Demo:**

- **Activity:**
- Demonstrations of various progress tracking apps and software are provided, showing how technology can support and monitor goal achievement.
- **Impact:**
- Employees learn how to use tech tools to keep their goals on track and dynamically adjust their strategies based on real-time feedback.

As the day concludes, Elena brings everyone together for a group reflection session. She encourages the team to share their goals and the insights gained through the activities. She emphasizes the ongoing support that OptiTech will provide to ensure that everyone has the resources and motivation to achieve their set goals.

The team leaves the workshop with a clear set of personally relevant goals and a renewed sense of purpose. They appreciate the structured approach to goal-setting and the practical tools provided to monitor their progress.

As the lights dim in the assembly hall, Elena watches her

team file out, their conversations buzzing with optimism and plans for the future. She feels a profound sense of satisfaction, knowing that the goal-setting skills they've honed today will not only enhance their performance but also contribute to OptiTech's growth and success in the competitive tech industry.

Intrinsic vs. Extrinsic Motivation

Building on the momentum from the goal-setting workshop, Elena organizes a specialized session to explore the differences between intrinsic and extrinsic motivation and how each influences employee behavior and satisfaction. OptiTech's large multi-purpose room is divided into two distinct zones: one decorated to evoke intrinsic motivations with art, literature, and personal achievement displays; the other designed to reflect extrinsic motivations with examples of bonuses, trophies, and public recognition accolades.

As OptiTech team members enter the multi-purpose room, they are struck by the stark contrast between the two zones. Each is designed to stimulate discussion and reflection on what truly motivates them at work. Elena, understanding the critical balance between these two forms of motivation, prepares to guide her team through a series of activities and discussions designed to reveal deeper insights into their own motivational drivers.

Elena's Introductory Talk: Elena begins the session with an engaging overview of intrinsic and extrinsic motivation, defining each and discussing their impact on workplace dynamics. She emphasizes the importance of understanding these motivations not just for personal growth but also for enhancing team synergy and productivity.

Interactive Activities:

1. **Intrinsic Motivation Zone:**

- **Activity:**
- Team members participate in activities like writing personal missions, creating vision boards, and discussing moments when they felt fulfilled at work without external rewards. This zone encourages reflection on personal growth, passion for work, and the joy derived from overcoming challenges.
- **Impact:**
- Employees explore how intrinsic motivators such as autonomy, mastery, and purpose drive their engagement and commitment to their work, potentially leading to greater innovation and persistence.

1. **Extrinsic Motivation Zone:**

- **Activity:**
- In this area, employees engage with scenarios involving promotions, pay raises, and company-wide recognition. They discuss how these rewards have influenced their work decisions and behaviors in the past.
- **Impact:**
- This zone highlights the role of external rewards in motivating employees, such as increasing immediate productivity or compliance, and helps employees understand the effectiveness and limitations of such motivators.

Group Discussion and Role Play:

- Elena facilitates a group discussion where team members compare their experiences in each zone. Following this, they role-play scenarios where they must motivate a colleague using both intrinsic and extrinsic motivators, highlighting the nuances and effectiveness of each approach in different situations.

Expert Panel Discussion:

- Elena invites a panel of motivational psychologists and seasoned corporate leaders who discuss the balance between intrinsic and extrinsic motivation in maintaining a motivated workforce. They provide insights into aligning corporate strategies with motivational needs and adapting leadership styles to foster a more motivating environment.

Elena's Concluding Reflections: As the session concludes, Elena gathers everyone for a final reflection. She asks the team to think about how they can apply their understanding of intrinsic and extrinsic motivations to enhance their own and their team's performance and satisfaction.

The team leaves the session with a deeper understanding of their personal and professional motivators. They recognize the importance of balancing intrinsic and extrinsic motivations to maintain a healthy, productive work environment.

As the room clears, Elena feels confident that her team is better equipped to harness their motivations effectively. This understanding, she believes, is key to building a resilient and dynamic team at OptiTech, poised to meet the challenges of the tech industry with enthusiasm and dedication.

The Role of Feedback in Motivating Employees

Following the exploration of intrinsic and extrinsic motivations, Elena identifies a critical element in sustaining motivation: feedback. To emphasize its importance and effectiveness, she transforms a section of OptiTech's training facility into an interactive feedback studio. The setup includes stations for giving and receiving feedback, equipped with recording devices, mirrors for self-reflection, and a variety of communication tools designed to simulate different feedback scenarios.

As the team assembles in the newly arranged feedback studio, there's an air of anticipation mixed with a bit of apprehension. Elena knows that while feedback is vital, it's often a sensitive area for many. She is prepared with a carefully crafted agenda that includes training on constructive feedback techniques, role-playing exercises, and expert talks on the psychology of feedback.

Elena's Introductory Speech: Elena opens the session with a passionate discussion about the power of feedback in driving personal growth and organizational success. She emphasizes that feedback, when done correctly, is a tremendous motivating force that can lead to increased performance, greater job satisfaction, and personal development.

Interactive Activities:

1. **Constructive Feedback Training:**

- **Activity:**
- Team members participate in a workshop led by a communication expert who teaches them how to give and receive constructive feedback. The training includes understanding the importance of timing, tone, and specificity.
- **Impact:**
- Employees learn to frame feedback in a way that is clear and motivational rather than critical or demoralizing.

1. **Feedback Role-Playing Station:**

- **Activity:**
- In this station, employees engage in role-playing exercises. They practice giving and receiving feedback based on past project experiences, using techniques learned in the previous workshop.
- **Impact:**
- Role-playing helps employees experience firsthand how different feedback approaches affect their reception and response, enhancing their understanding of effective communication.

1. **Real-Time Feedback Session:**

- **Activity:**
- Employees use apps and devices to record and review their practice feedback sessions. This technology pro-

vides them with immediate feedback on their delivery and demeanor.
- **Impact:**
- This direct and immediate form of feedback allows team members to quickly adjust and improve their communication styles.

Expert Panel Discussion:

- Elena invites a panel consisting of a psychologist, a seasoned HR professional, and a successful startup CEO to discuss the role of feedback in motivating employees. The panel explores various feedback mechanisms, including peer-to-peer feedback, digital feedback tools, and 360-degree reviews.
- **Impact:**
- The discussion provides deeper insights into how effectively implemented feedback cultures can drive engagement and motivation across all levels of an organization.

Elena's Concluding Reflections: As the session wraps up, Elena brings everyone together for a group reflection. She highlights key takeaways and encourages her team to integrate these feedback techniques into their daily interactions and annual reviews.

The team leaves the studio feeling empowered and motivated, with a new appreciation for feedback as a tool for professional growth and enhancement of workplace dynamics.

Watching her team engage with new concepts and tools, Elena is confident that the improved feedback mechanisms will foster a more transparent, communicative, and ultimately more motivated work environment at OptiTech. This session marks a significant step forward in building a culture that values and utilizes feedback to propel both individual and company-wide success.

Developing Motivational Strategies for Diverse Teams

With a deeper understanding of feedback mechanisms firmly in place, Elena shifts her focus to the challenge of motivating a diverse workforce. She organizes a strategic planning session in OptiTech's main conference hall, now set up as a vibrant workshop space with areas designated for small group brainstorming, large discussion panels, and interactive digital displays showcasing motivational strategies from around the world.

The diversity of OptiTech's team, with members from various cultural backgrounds, age groups, and professional disciplines, presents unique challenges and opportunities for motivation. Elena, aware of the nuances involved, prepares a multifaceted session designed to develop customized motivational strategies that resonate across this varied employee base.

Elena begins the session by emphasizing the importance of recognizing and celebrating the diversity within their team. She explains that today's activities are aimed at harnessing this diversity to create a motivational environment that supports all team members uniquely and effectively.

Interactive Activities:

1. **Cultural Sensitivity Workshop:**

- **Activity:**
- A cultural consultant conducts a workshop on cultural sensitivity in the workplace, highlighting how cultural differences can influence motivational needs and responses.
- **Impact:**
- Team members gain insights into various cultural perspectives on motivation, learning to appreciate and incorporate these differences into team dynamics and leadership approaches.

1. **Generational Motivation Panel:**

- **Activity:**
- A panel discussion featuring representatives from different age groups at OptiTech, discussing what motivates them at work, from career advancement and job security to work-life balance and social impact.
- **Impact:**
- Understanding generational differences helps Elena and her managers tailor motivational strategies to meet the varied needs and expectations of their multigenerational workforce.

1. **Interactive Motivation Labs:**

- **Activity:**
- Teams rotate through stations equipped with interactive

tools to design specific motivational strategies for hypothetical scenarios involving diverse team compositions.
- **Impact:**
- Participants apply their learning in real-time, experimenting with and refining a variety of motivational techniques, such as flexible work arrangements, personalized recognition programs, and team-building activities that celebrate cultural diversity.

Expert-Led Innovation Sprint:

- Elena introduces an innovation sprint led by a renowned motivational psychologist who guides the team through a rapid prototyping session to develop new, creative motivational tools and programs.
- **Impact:**
- The sprint fosters a hands-on approach to innovation in motivation, encouraging creativity and immediate feedback, which leads to the development of practical and innovative motivation solutions tailored to diverse needs.

As the session concludes, Elena gathers all participants for a final reflection. She encourages her team to continue the dialogue and exploration started today and to actively seek out and implement motivational strategies that are inclusive and effective.

The team leaves the session equipped with not only a deeper understanding of the diverse motivational needs within their ranks but also with practical strategies and tools designed to meet these needs. They feel empowered to contribute to a workplace environment that is actively inclusive and dynamically motivated.

Elena watches her team disperse, energized by the day's activities and discussions. She is confident that the commitment to developing motivational strategies that acknowledge and celebrate diversity will lead to a stronger, more cohesive, and highly motivated team at OptiTech, poised to innovate and excel in the competitive tech landscape.

4

Chapter 4: Communication in Organizations

Building on the lessons and strategies developed in earlier workshops, Elena turns her focus to enhancing communication within OptiTech. Understanding that effective communication is vital for maintaining motivation and ensuring clarity in a dynamic workplace, she arranges a day-long retreat at a serene, secluded venue near the coastline, ideal for open dialogues and reflective learning. The venue is equipped with various communication enhancement tools and stations designed to practice and simulate different communication styles and challenges.

As the OptiTech team arrives at the coastal retreat, the sound of waves crashing and gulls calling sets a calming backdrop, perfect for the day's goals. Today, Elena plans to break down communication barriers and build a stronger, more coherent communication flow within the diverse team at OptiTech.

With the sea breeze gently blowing through the open pavilion, Elena opens the retreat by emphasizing the importance of communication in building and maintaining a healthy organizational culture. She outlines the day's activities, which are crafted to explore various aspects of effective communication, from listening skills to non-verbal cues, and to address specific communication issues that have arisen within OptiTech.

Interactive Activities:

1. **The Communication Process Workshop:**

- **Activity:**
- A communication expert leads a workshop on the elements of the communication process, including encoding, medium choice, decoding, and feedback. Participants engage in exercises that illustrate common breakdowns in each stage.
- **Impact:**
- Understanding the complexities of communication helps team members identify where misunderstandings typically occur and how to address them effectively.

1. **Non-Verbal Communication Zone:**

- **Activity:**
- This zone focuses on the power of non-verbal cues such as body language, eye contact, and tone of voice. Through role-playing, participants experience how non-verbal communication can change the message being conveyed.
- **Impact:**
- Employees become more aware of their own body lan-

guage and learn to read others' non-verbal signals, enhancing their ability to communicate with empathy and clarity.

1. **Digital Communication Challenges:**

- **Activity:**
- In this session, teams tackle common challenges in digital communication, such as email tone misunderstandings and instant messaging etiquette. They learn about tools and techniques to improve clarity and prevent conflicts in remote communication settings.
- **Impact:**
- As OptiTech relies heavily on digital tools, improving these skills is critical for ensuring that team members feel connected and understood, even when not physically present.

1. **Cross-Cultural Communication Workshop:**

- **Activity:**
- Recognizing the diversity within their team, this workshop addresses cultural differences that impact communication styles and preferences. It includes discussions and scenarios that expose team members to a variety of cultural communication norms and taboos.
- **Impact:**
- This enhances sensitivity and adaptability, fostering a more inclusive and respectful workplace environment.

At sunset, with the team gathered around a bonfire on the

beach, Elena facilitates a closing circle where participants share their insights and commitments to improve communication within their teams. She stresses the ongoing nature of communication improvement and the need for continuous practice and openness to feedback.

The team leaves the retreat with a renewed appreciation for the complexities of effective communication and armed with practical tools and strategies to enhance their daily interactions. They feel more connected as a team and more competent as communicators, ready to apply these skills to enhance collaboration and efficiency at OptiTech.

As the retreat ends and the team heads back to the city, the calm confidence and understanding reflected in their interactions show that today's activities have not only strengthened their communication skills but also their bonds as teammates. Elena feels a deep sense of accomplishment, knowing that strong communication is the backbone of a thriving organizational culture and she has set her team on the right path.

The Communication Process: Models and Barriers

With the tranquil backdrop of the coastal retreat still fresh in their minds, Elena decides to bring the lessons closer to home at OptiTech's headquarters. She transforms a conference room into an interactive learning center where various models of communication are visually displayed around the room. Each station is set up to demonstrate common communication barriers and how they can be overcome.

As team members enter the revamped conference room, they find it segmented into different areas, each representing a specific communication model and associated barriers. This setting is designed to provide a hands-on understanding of how communication flows within an organization and how it can be disrupted. Elena, keen on reinforcing the importance of effective communication, prepares to guide her team through understanding and overcoming these barriers.

Elena's Introduction to the Workshop: Elena starts the session by explaining the significance of understanding the communication process in depth. She points out that by mastering this, the team can enhance both their interpersonal communications and their collaborative efforts on projects. She introduces the first model of communication, setting the stage for a day of deep learning and interactive problem-solving.

Interactive Activities:

1. **Linear Model Station:**

   - **Activity:**
   - Participants explore the linear model of communication, where information flows in one direction from the sender to the receiver. Role-playing exercises simulate the absence of feedback, highlighting potential misunderstandings.
   - **Impact:**
   - This activity helps team members understand the limitations of one-way communication, especially in a fast-paced tech environment where feedback is crucial to success.

1. **Interactive Model Station:**

- **Activity:**
- This station demonstrates the interactive model, which incorporates feedback, allowing for back-and-forth communication between sender and receiver. Participants engage in activities that involve giving and receiving feedback on specific tasks.
- **Impact:**
- By experiencing real-time feedback, employees learn the importance of adjusting messages based on the responses of others, improving clarity and understanding.

1. **Transactional Model Station:**

- **Activity:**
- The transactional model is presented, emphasizing the dynamic and simultaneous nature of communication where all parties are both senders and receivers. Simulation games are used to showcase this model in action, focusing on the fluidity and ongoing adjustments in communication.
- **Impact:**
- Participants gain insights into how communication can evolve within a conversation, learning to adapt quickly and more effectively to others' inputs.

1. **Barriers to Effective Communication:**

- **Activity:**
- A section of the room is dedicated to identifying and overcoming common communication barriers such as jargon, noise, emotional barriers, and cultural differ-

ences. Through interactive quizzes and troubleshooting scenarios, team members identify barriers they have encountered and work together to find solutions.
- **Impact:**
- Understanding these barriers and how to overcome them equips the team with the skills to enhance their daily interactions and prevent common communication pitfalls.

Elena's Conclusive Discussion: To wrap up the workshop, Elena facilitates a group discussion where participants share their experiences from each station and commit to specific actions they will take to improve communication within their teams. She emphasizes the interconnected nature of communication models and barriers, encouraging ongoing vigilance and proactive management.

The team leaves the session with a comprehensive understanding of the communication process and a toolkit for identifying and addressing barriers. They feel empowered to communicate more effectively, equipped with new strategies that are immediately applicable in their work.

As the team disperses, there's a palpable sense of commitment to breaking down barriers and fostering an environment of open and effective communication. Elena watches her team leave, confident that the insights gained today will lead to improved project outcomes and a more harmonious workplace at OptiTech.

Non-verbal Communication and Its Impact

Fresh from the insights gained on the communication models and barriers, Elena decides to delve into the often-overlooked aspect of communication—non-verbal cues. Understanding its critical impact on interpersonal interactions, she sets up the next workshop in OptiTech's atrium, a space with clear glass walls that foster an open atmosphere. The space is equipped with mirrors, video recording equipment, and playback screens to facilitate self-observation and analysis.

As team members step into the brightly lit atrium, they are met with stations designed to teach and test their non-verbal communication skills. Elena, aware of the subtleties and power of non-verbal cues, prepares to guide her team through exercises that reveal how much of their communication is conveyed without words.

Elena begins the workshop with a compelling demonstration of non-verbal communication, showing a silent video of a recent team meeting and asking participants to interpret the interactions based on body language, facial expressions, and gestures alone. This eye-opening introduction sets the tone for the importance of non-verbal cues in effective communication.

Interactive Activities:

1. **Mirror Exercises:**

- **Activity:**
- Participants are asked to deliver a short speech about their current projects while observing themselves in a mirror.

Focus is on their body language, facial expressions, and eye movements.
- **Impact:**
- This self-observation helps team members become more aware of their own non-verbal signals and how they might be perceived by others.

1. **Video Analysis Station:**

- **Activity:**
- Teams record themselves in a simulated project update meeting. They then review the video to identify non-verbal cues and discuss how these might have influenced the meeting's outcomes.
- **Impact:**
- Reviewing their behaviors on video helps participants understand the significant role their non-verbal communication plays in supporting or undermining their verbal messages.

1. **Role-Playing for Empathy Building:**

- **Activity:**
- Participants engage in role-playing exercises where they must communicate without speaking, using only gestures, facial expressions, and body language to convey their messages.
- **Impact:**
- This exercise enhances their ability to read and use non-verbal cues effectively, building empathy and improving their capacity to communicate with those who may

speak different languages or come from different cultural backgrounds.

1. **Expert-Led Seminar on Cultural Variations:**

- **Activity:**
- A communication expert discusses the cultural variations in non-verbal communication, illustrating how gestures acceptable in one culture might be offensive or misunderstood in another.
- **Impact:**
- This seminar broadens the team's understanding of global communication practices, which is crucial for a diverse company like OptiTech that interacts on an international scale.

As the day concludes, Elena gathers everyone for a reflection session where they share personal insights and revelations from the day's activities. She emphasizes the integration of non-verbal communication awareness into their daily interactions and the overall communication strategy at OptiTech.

The team leaves the workshop with a heightened awareness of their non-verbal communication and its impact. They feel better equipped to interact in a way that conveys respect, understanding, and clarity, regardless of the spoken content.

Watching her team interact as they leave the atrium, Elena notices immediate improvements in their body language and engagement with each other. She is satisfied knowing that these subtle yet powerful aspects of communication are no longer underappreciated at OptiTech, fostering a more nuanced and effective communication environment.

Digital Communication and Organizational Behavior

After a profound exploration into non-verbal communication, Elena pivots to a topic of growing importance in OptiTech's day-to-day operations: digital communication. She sets up a "Digital Communication Hub" in one of the company's tech-forward conference rooms, equipped with the latest in collaborative software, digital whiteboards, and communication platforms. This session is designed to address the nuances of digital interactions and their impact on organizational behavior.

As team members enter the Digital Communication Hub, they're greeted by stations each themed around different digital communication tools such as Slack, Zoom, and Microsoft Teams. The room buzzes with a sense of modernity and efficiency. Elena, recognizing the critical role of digital tools in today's workplace, prepares to guide the team through the complexities of virtual communication and its behavioral implications.

Elena's Introductory Presentation: Elena opens the session by underscoring the importance of mastering digital communication to enhance operational effectiveness and maintain organizational cohesion in a tech-centric environment. She illustrates how miscommunications in digital formats can lead to conflicts and misunderstandings, affecting overall productivity and workplace atmosphere.

Interactive Activities:

1. **Email Communication Workshop:**

- **Activity:**
- Participants engage in crafting emails under various scenarios—addressing a conflict, announcing changes, requesting information. Their emails are then critiqued in real-time by communication experts.
- **Impact:**
- This helps team members refine their ability to convey tone and clarity in email communications, reducing the potential for misinterpretation.

1. **Instant Messaging Etiquette Game:**

- **Activity:**
- A gamified setup where participants respond to instant messages in a race against the clock, emphasizing the need for quick, clear, and respectful responses.
- **Impact:**
- This activity underscores the importance of maintaining professionalism and courtesy in rapid communication environments, enhancing responsiveness without sacrificing politeness or clarity.

1. **Video Call Role-Playing:**

- **Activity:**
- Teams participate in simulated video calls where they must handle various communication challenges, such as

dealing with technical difficulties, ensuring participatory balance, and managing cross-cultural misunderstandings.
- **Impact:**
- Role-playing in this context prepares employees for the complexities of video conferencing, a mainstay in modern business communication, fostering better preparedness and adaptability.

1. **Interactive Lecture on Communication Platforms:**

- **Activity:**
- A tech communication expert presents an interactive lecture on choosing the right digital tools for different communication needs and integrating them seamlessly into daily operations.
- **Impact:**
- This educates the team on the strategic use of digital tools to enhance communication effectiveness and team collaboration across geographical and functional boundaries.

Elena wraps up the session by facilitating a discussion on the best practices learned and how they can be applied within OptiTech. She encourages the team to always consider the human aspect behind the digital screen, promoting empathy and patience.

The team leaves the Digital Communication Hub equipped with advanced skills in digital communication, a deep understanding of its impacts on organizational behavior, and a commitment to applying these practices to improve everyday interactions.

As Elena watches her team leave, energized and chatting about the new tools and techniques they've learned, she feels confident that OptiTech is better prepared to thrive in a digital communication-driven world. This step forward not only strengthens their internal operations but also enhances their ability to communicate effectively with clients and stakeholders across the digital landscape.

Cross-Cultural Communication Challenges

After exploring the intricacies of digital communication, Elena shifts her focus to a topic crucial for OptiTech's global operations: cross-cultural communication. She organizes a "Global Communication Day" in the company's largest auditorium, transforming it into a cultural fair with booths representing the various countries and cultures within the OptiTech team. This immersive environment is designed to highlight the challenges and rewards of effective cross-cultural communication.

As team members enter the auditorium, they are greeted by a vibrant array of cultural displays, each offering insights into different communication styles, etiquette, and values from around the world. Elena, understanding the complexity and importance of navigating cultural differences in a global marketplace, prepares to guide her team through a series of activities designed to enhance their cultural competence and communication skills.

Elena's Opening Remarks: Elena begins the day with a powerful address about the value of diversity at OptiTech and the critical role that effective cross-cultural communication plays in fostering a collaborative and inclusive workplace.

She stresses the importance of empathy, respect, and understanding in overcoming cultural barriers to communication.

Interactive Activities:

1. **Cultural Simulation Workshops:**

- **Activity:**
- Team members participate in role-playing scenarios that simulate business meetings with partners from different cultural backgrounds. These simulations include negotiating contracts, resolving conflicts, and conducting presentations.
- **Impact:**
- Participants experience firsthand the potential misunderstandings that can arise from cultural differences and practice strategies to navigate them effectively.

1. **Language Barrier Exercises:**

- **Activity:**
- In this challenging exercise, teams must communicate task instructions in a language not native to any member, highlighting the difficulties and frustrations that can arise from language barriers.
- **Impact:**
- This activity fosters greater empathy for non-native speakers and illustrates the importance of clear, simple communication in a multicultural environment.

1. **Cultural Etiquette Quiz Games:**

- **Activity:**
- Teams compete in a quiz format to answer questions about business etiquette, communication preferences, and taboos across different cultures represented at OptiTech.
- **Impact:**
- Quizzes help solidify knowledge of diverse cultural norms and practices, reducing the risk of accidental offenses in real-world interactions.

1. **Expert Panel Discussion on Global Business Communication:**

- **Activity:**
- A panel of cultural communication experts discusses best practices for global business interactions, sharing insights from their experiences and answering questions from OptiTech employees.
- **Impact:**
- The discussion provides actionable advice on building effective, respectful, and sensitive communication strategies that can be applied across various cultural contexts.

Elena concludes the event by facilitating a reflective discussion among the participants, encouraging them to share their learnings and how they can apply these insights to their daily work and global interactions. She emphasizes the ongoing journey of cultural learning and adaptation required in a globalized world.

The team leaves the event with a deeper understanding and appreciation of the nuances of cross-cultural communication.

They are more aware of the potential challenges and equipped with the tools and strategies to build stronger, more effective relationships with international colleagues and clients.

As the auditorium empties, Elena feels a profound sense of accomplishment. She watches her team, now more culturally aware and communicatively skilled, ready to navigate the complexities of a global business environment with confidence and sensitivity. This day marks a significant step forward in strengthening OptiTech's position as a culturally competent and globally savvy tech leader.

Communication Networks within Organizations

Building on the success of the Global Communication Day, Elena recognizes the need to enhance the internal communication networks at OptiTech to ensure seamless information flow and collaboration across departments. To tackle this, she organizes a "Network Optimization Workshop" in OptiTech's state-of-the-art collaborative space, which is equipped with digital network mapping tools, interactive displays, and communication technology setups.

As team members gather in the collaborative space, they find it transformed into an interactive lab designed to visualize and optimize the flow of information within OptiTech. Elena, aware that effective communication networks are the backbone of any thriving organization, prepares to guide her team through understanding and refining these networks.

Elena begins the workshop with an engaging presentation on the importance of robust communication networks and how they can dramatically improve efficiency and innovation. She explains different types of communication networks—

chain, wheel, all-channel—and the contexts in which they are most effective.

Interactive Activities:

1. **Communication Network Mapping:**

- **Activity:**
- Teams use digital tools to map out the existing communication networks within their departments, identifying key nodes, links, and any apparent bottlenecks or gaps in the flow of information.
- **Impact:**
- This visualization helps team members understand the structure and effectiveness of their current communication practices, highlighting areas for improvement.

1. **Network Re-design Simulation:**

- **Activity:**
- Using the insights gained from the mapping activity, teams simulate different network models to determine which configuration best supports their specific communication needs. They experiment with changing the central nodes and paths of information flow.
- **Impact:**
- Teams can practically assess the impact of different network structures on communication efficiency and team performance, allowing them to make informed decisions about restructuring their networks.

1. **Technology Integration Session:**

- **Activity:**
- An IT specialist presents the latest communication technologies and software that can support or enhance organizational networks, such as collaborative platforms and project management tools.
- **Impact:**
- By integrating advanced technologies into their communication networks, teams can improve real-time communication and collaboration across geographic and functional boundaries.

1. **Role-Playing for Conflict Resolution:**

- **Activity:**
- In role-playing scenarios, team members practice resolving conflicts that arise from miscommunications within their newly designed networks, focusing on maintaining clear and open channels of dialogue.
- **Impact:**
- This exercise helps team members develop the skills to quickly and effectively address communication issues, ensuring that network changes lead to positive outcomes.

As the workshop concludes, Elena brings everyone together for a discussion on the new network designs and the planned implementations. She emphasizes the importance of ongoing assessment and adaptation of communication networks to keep pace with organizational growth and change.

The team leaves the workshop with a clear plan for enhancing their communication networks, equipped with new tools and strategies to foster a more connected and communicative organization.

Watching her team engaged and proactive about implementing these new communication structures, Elena feels confident that OptiTech is on the right path to becoming more integrated and responsive. This development not only promises to improve operational efficiency but also strengthens the internal bonds within the company, paving the way for greater innovation and success.

Strategies to Improve Communication Effectiveness

Following the successful workshop on optimizing communication networks, Elena plans a comprehensive session focused on implementing strategies that will enhance communication effectiveness across OptiTech. She transforms one of the larger conference rooms into a "Communication Strategy Lab," where each corner is dedicated to different strategic elements such as clarity, feedback loops, communication tools, and training modules.

As team members enter the Communication Strategy Lab, they're greeted by a series of interactive stations, each designed to deepen their understanding and mastery of effective communication strategies. Elena, committed to equipping her team with the tools they need to communicate more effectively, has prepared a series of activities that will engage and challenge the team in real-world communication scenarios.

Elena's Introductory Overview: Elena opens the session with a brief overview of why communication fails and how strategic improvements can drastically enhance productivity and employee satisfaction. She introduces the key strategies they will explore and practice during the session, emphasizing the impact of effective communication on achieving OptiTech's organizational goals.

Interactive Activities:

1. **Clarity Workshops:**

- **Activity:**
- Participants engage in crafting and delivering clear, concise messages through various mediums—email, presentations, and team meetings. Coaches provide feedback on their clarity and suggest improvements.
- **Impact:**
- This station helps team members refine their ability to convey information succinctly and clearly, reducing potential misunderstandings and increasing overall communication efficiency.

1. **Feedback Loop Simulations:**

- **Activity:**
- Teams participate in simulations that emphasize the importance of constructive feedback. They practice giving and receiving feedback in different scenarios, learning how to integrate feedback into daily communication practices.
- **Impact:**
- This enhances the team's ability to use feedback as a tool

for continuous improvement and encourages a culture of open communication and growth.

1. **Digital Communication Tools Exploration:**

- **Activity:**
- A tech showcase demonstrates the latest communication tools and platforms that can facilitate better collaboration and information sharing. Team members test these tools in guided sessions.
- **Impact:**
- By familiarizing themselves with cutting-edge communication technology, team members can choose the most effective tools to support their specific needs, improving connectivity and workflow.

1. **Cultural Competence and Empathy Building:**

- **Activity:**
- This station focuses on enhancing empathy and cultural competence through role-playing exercises and scenario-based learning, addressing communication across different cultures and contexts within the company.
- **Impact:**
- Improving cultural competence and empathy helps prevent cultural misunderstandings and builds a more inclusive and supportive workplace environment.

At the close of the session, Elena gathers all participants for a group reflection. She encourages them to share insights gained and to commit to specific strategies they will implement in their teams. She highlights the importance of these strategies in driving OptiTech's mission and vision forward.

The team leaves the session equipped with practical strategies to enhance their communication effectiveness. They feel empowered with new skills and tools that promise to make their interactions more productive and fulfilling.

As Elena watches her team discuss their next steps and exchange ideas with renewed enthusiasm, she is confident that the improvements in communication will lead to greater innovation and collaboration across OptiTech. This session has not only provided the team with valuable tools but also reinforced the foundational role that effective communication plays in the success of the organization.

5

Chapter 5: Group Dynamics and Teamwork

Buoyed by the success of the communication strategies session, Elena recognizes the importance of addressing group dynamics and teamwork next. She organizes an intensive two-day offsite retreat at a scenic lodge surrounded by nature, perfect for team-building exercises and deep discussions. The retreat is designed to foster trust, cooperation, and understanding among team members from different departments within OptiTech.

As the OptiTech team arrives at the tranquil, forest-surrounded lodge, they are struck by the peace and beauty of the setting—a stark contrast to their bustling tech environment. The retreat promises a blend of structured activities and free time, allowing for both guided teamwork exercises and informal bonding. Elena, understanding the complexity of group dynamics, has curated a program to enhance teamwork through a series of collaborative challenges and reflective sessions.

Elena's Opening Remarks: Elena opens the retreat with a

fireside chat on the first evening, discussing the importance of effective teamwork and positive group dynamics in achieving organizational goals. She sets the tone for open communication and mutual support, encouraging everyone to participate fully and share openly during the retreat.

Interactive Activities:

1. **Team-Building Challenges:**

- **Activity:**
- Teams face off in a series of outdoor challenges designed to test and improve their problem-solving, communication, and cooperation skills. These include a high-ropes course, a navigation challenge, and a raft-building competition on the lake.
- **Impact:**
- These physically engaging activities help break down personal barriers and build trust among team members, showing how each person's strengths can contribute to common goals.

1. **Leadership Rotation Exercises:**

- **Activity:**
- Each team member takes turns leading the group through various less physically demanding tasks, such as cooking a meal or organizing a group discussion about the company's future.
- **Impact:**
- This exercise gives everyone a chance to experience lead-

ership roles and empowers them to showcase and develop their leadership qualities in a supportive environment.

1. **Stages of Group Development Workshop:**

- **Activity:**
- A facilitator leads a workshop on the Tuckman model of group development: forming, storming, norming, and performing. Teams assess what stage they are currently in and discuss strategies to move towards "performing."
- **Impact:**
- Understanding the developmental stages of a team allows members to identify and address issues that may be holding them back, facilitating smoother collaboration.

1. **Conflict Resolution Role-Play:**

- **Activity:**
- Team members engage in role-playing scenarios that involve resolving hypothetical conflicts within their teams, guided by a conflict resolution expert.
- **Impact:**
- These role-plays equip team members with practical tools for managing and resolving conflicts constructively, thereby strengthening group cohesion.

At the end of the retreat, around the warmth of a closing bonfire, Elena invites everyone to reflect on their experiences and share their takeaways. She emphasizes the continuous nature of team development and the need for ongoing effort to maintain healthy group dynamics.

The team leaves the retreat feeling more connected as a unit and better equipped to work together effectively. They have a deeper understanding of each other's strengths, weaknesses, and communication styles, which fosters greater empathy and collaboration back at the office.

As the team packs up to leave the lodge, there's a noticeable difference in their interactions—more laughter, more helping hands, more understanding. Elena watches with satisfaction, knowing that the seeds planted during this retreat will grow into stronger team dynamics and enhanced teamwork at OptiTech, propelling the company toward its strategic goals with renewed vigor.

Stages of Group Development

Energized by the success of the initial retreat activities, Elena decides to delve deeper into the Tuckman model of group development during the second day of the offsite. She transforms a spacious conference room at the lodge into an interactive learning environment, with stations designed to simulate each stage of group development: Forming, Storming, Norming, and Performing. The setting includes visual aids, role-playing scripts, and facilitator-led discussion areas.

As the sun rises over the tranquil retreat, the OptiTech team gathers in the newly arranged conference room. The air buzzes with anticipation as team members prepare to engage with the Tuckman model, exploring how their teams can evolve and enhance their collaboration. Elena, aware of the transformative potential of understanding these stages, is ready to guide her team through this critical exploration.

Elena starts the day with an engaging overview of the Tuckman model, explaining each stage's significance and typical behaviors. She emphasizes the natural progression most teams experience and encourages the team to embrace these stages as growth opportunities.

Interactive Activities:

1. **Forming Stage Simulation:**

- **Activity:**
- Team members are reshuffled to form new groups, simulating the 'Forming' stage where everything is new, and members are polite but distant. They engage in ice-breaking activities designed to introduce members to one another and start building initial connections.
- **Impact:**
- This simulation helps participants understand the cautious optimism and superficial interactions typical of newly formed teams and the importance of setting a positive tone from the beginning.

1. **Storming Stage Role-Play:**

- **Activity:**
- In their new groups, members now tackle a challenging project task, designed to bring out conflicts and differences in opinions, mimicking the 'Storming' stage. Facilitators observe and guide the discussions to prevent real discord while highlighting the learning points.
- **Impact:**

- Participants experience the inevitable conflicts that arise as team members start to push boundaries and assert individual ideas, learning strategies to navigate these conflicts constructively.

1. **Norming Stage Workshop:**

- **Activity:**
- Following the resolution of the storming stage, teams discuss and establish norms and agreements on how to work together effectively, entering the 'Norming' stage. They create a team charter that outlines agreed-upon rules and roles.
- **Impact:**
- This workshop helps teams develop a collective identity and mutual respect, with clear expectations and processes that facilitate smoother interactions.

1. **Performing Stage Challenge:**

- **Activity:**
- Teams now apply all they have learned to perform a complex task under time pressure, showcasing the 'Performing' stage where high levels of autonomy, trust, and alignment drive superior performance and achievement.
- **Impact:**
- This challenge demonstrates how effectively developed teams can solve problems and deliver results, highlighting the efficiency and creativity that come with reaching this stage.

As the day wraps up, Elena gathers everyone for a final reflection circle. She invites feedback on the day's activities and discusses how understanding these stages can help each team member contribute to their team's development proactively.

The team leaves the session with a deep understanding of the stages of group development and practical experience navigating each phase. They feel better prepared to support their teams through these stages back at OptiTech.

Watching her team interact with newfound understanding and commitment, Elena feels a profound sense of accomplishment. She knows that equipping her team with the knowledge and skills to navigate group development stages is essential for fostering a collaborative, innovative, and high-performing organizational culture.

The Role of Leadership in Teams

Inspired by the progress made during the exploration of group development stages, Elena shifts the focus to the pivotal role of leadership in teams. She organizes a dedicated session at OptiTech's headquarters, transforming the main auditorium into a leadership lab, complete with stations for different leadership styles and scenarios. The setup is designed to explore how various leadership approaches impact team dynamics and performance.

As OptiTech team members filter into the auditorium, they find themselves surrounded by various interactive setups, each representing a different leadership theory—transformational, transactional, and situational leadership. Elena, understanding the critical influence of effective leadership on team success, has planned a series of activities that will challenge and enhance the team's leadership skills.

Elena opens the session by emphasizing the significant impact that leaders have on their teams, not just in terms of guiding them towards goals but also in shaping the team's culture and resolving conflicts. She introduces the concept of adaptive leadership—tailoring leadership styles to the needs of the team and individual situations.

Interactive Activities:

1. **Transformational Leadership Workshop:**

- **Activity:**
- Participants rotate through a scenario where they must lead a team through a transformative change process, focusing on inspiring and motivating their team to embrace a new vision. The exercise involves role-playing, feedback, and reflection.
- **Impact:**
- This workshop helps participants understand how transformational leadership can inspire and elevate team performance through empowerment and by aligning team goals with broader organizational visions.

1. **Transactional Leadership Challenge:**

- **Activity:**
- In this station, team members experience leading a team under transactional leadership, focusing on structured tasks, clear rewards, and penalties. They manage a

simulated project where they must achieve specific results within set parameters.
- **Impact:**
- Participants learn the benefits and limitations of a transactional approach, particularly in scenarios requiring high levels of control and adherence to processes.

1. **Situational Leadership Role-Play:**

- **Activity:**
- Teams engage in role-playing exercises that require leaders to adapt their style to the developmental level of their team members. Scenarios vary from leading inexperienced teams needing guidance to empowering experienced teams to innovate.
- **Impact:**
- This activity underscores the flexibility required in leadership, demonstrating how different situations might require different leadership responses for optimal team outcomes.

1. **Leadership Reflection Zone:**

- **Activity:**
- At this station, participants reflect on their experiences at each leadership station, journaling about what styles resonated with them, what challenges they faced, and how they can apply these insights to their real-world team interactions.
- **Impact:**
- Reflection helps solidify learning, allowing leaders to

consciously integrate effective leadership practices into their daily management of teams.

Elena concludes the session by bringing everyone together for a group debrief. She discusses how the different leadership styles can be integrated and adapted to suit the unique needs of teams at OptiTech. She encourages ongoing learning and adaptation in leadership approaches.

The team leaves the session with a nuanced understanding of how various leadership styles can influence team dynamics and with the skills to adapt their approaches based on team needs and organizational goals.

As the auditorium doors close behind the departing team, Elena feels confident that the insights gained today will lead to stronger, more effective leadership across OptiTech. By understanding and applying diverse leadership styles, OptiTech's leaders are better equipped to foster a collaborative, innovative, and dynamic work environment.

Conflict Resolution Strategies

Following the deep dive into leadership's role in team dynamics, Elena organizes a crucial session focused on conflict resolution strategies. Recognizing that conflict is inevitable in a dynamic workplace like OptiTech, she converts a large conference room into a "Conflict Resolution Arena," where realistic conflict scenarios will be staged, and different resolution strategies will be tested and discussed.

As team members enter the Conflict Resolution Arena, they find the room divided into several stations, each representing common workplace conflicts: interpersonal disagreements, project management clashes, resource allocation issues, and strategic direction debates. Elena, aware that effective conflict resolution is key to maintaining a productive and harmonious work environment, has prepared a program that will equip her team with the tools to manage and resolve conflicts constructively.

Elena's Opening Remarks: Elena begins the session by discussing the nature of conflict in organizations and its dual role as both a potential disruptor and a catalyst for innovation and growth. She emphasizes the importance of addressing conflicts constructively and introduces the various conflict resolution strategies that will be explored throughout the day.

Interactive Activities:

1. **Role-Playing Conflict Scenarios:**

   - **Activity:**
   - Teams rotate through different stations where they engage in role-playing exercises that simulate specific types of conflicts. Trained facilitators observe and guide the discussions, providing feedback and tips on handling each situation.
   - **Impact:**
   - These role-plays help participants experience conflicts firsthand and practice applying conflict resolution strategies such as negotiation, mediation, and compromise in a controlled environment.

1. **Negotiation Workshop:**

- **Activity:**
- A negotiation expert conducts a workshop focusing on effective negotiation techniques that can lead to win-win outcomes. Participants learn about the principles of collaborative negotiation and practice these techniques in mock negotiation sessions.
- **Impact:**
- This workshop enhances participants' negotiation skills, an essential component of conflict resolution, helping them to reach agreements that satisfy all parties involved.

1. **Mediation Training:**

- **Activity:**
- Participants receive training on how to act as mediators in conflicts between other team members. They learn about the mediation process, including how to remain neutral, facilitate dialogue, and help disputing parties reach a resolution.
- **Impact:**
- Equipping team members with mediation skills empowers them to assist in resolving disputes within their teams, promoting a more collaborative and supportive work environment.

1. **Conflict Resolution Panel Discussion:**

- **Activity:**
- A panel of HR professionals and conflict resolution experts share their experiences and best practices for managing workplace conflicts. The discussion includes

a Q&A session where participants can seek advice on specific challenges they face.
- **Impact:**
- This discussion provides additional insights and strategies for handling complex conflicts, reinforcing the training received throughout the day.

As the session concludes, Elena gathers the team for a debriefing session. She invites participants to share their experiences and key takeaways from the day's activities. Elena stresses the ongoing nature of conflict resolution and encourages her team to continue practicing the skills they've learned.

The team leaves the session with a comprehensive understanding of conflict resolution strategies and practical experience in applying these strategies. They feel more confident in their ability to handle conflicts effectively, which is critical for maintaining team cohesion and productivity.

Watching her team interact with newfound understanding and skills, Elena feels reassured that OptiTech is better prepared to handle the inevitable challenges that arise from workplace conflicts. She is confident that the tools and strategies discussed today will help foster a more positive and collaborative work environment.

The Impact of Groupthink and How to Avoid It

Following a comprehensive exploration of conflict resolution strategies, Elena pivots to address a more subtle yet potentially detrimental issue impacting team dynamics: groupthink. Determined to cultivate a culture where diverse ideas thrive and decision-making is robust, she organizes a "Critical Thinking Workshop" in one of OptiTech's collaborative spaces. This space is meticulously arranged to facilitate independent thinking and constructive dissent, with stations for scenario analysis, debate, and reflective thinking.

As the OptiTech team gathers in the transformed workshop space, they find an atmosphere designed to challenge conventional thinking and encourage intellectual independence. Elena, aware of the risks posed by groupthink to innovation and effective decision-making, prepares to guide her team through activities that promote awareness and provide strategies to mitigate this phenomenon.

Elena begins the session by explaining the concept of groupthink—where the desire for harmony or conformity in a group results in an irrational or dysfunctional decision-making outcome. She emphasizes how groupthink can stifle innovation and lead to flawed outcomes, and introduces the day's activities designed to empower individuals to share diverse opinions and challenge the status quo.

Interactive Activities:

1. **Historical Case Study Reviews:**

- **Activity:**
- Teams review and discuss well-known historical instances of groupthink, such as the Bay of Pigs invasion and the Challenger space shuttle disaster. They analyze the causes, the impacts, and what could have been done differently.
- **Impact:**

- This activity highlights the severe consequences of groupthink, making the concept tangible and underscoring the importance of avoiding such dynamics in their own work.

1. **Role-Playing Dissent:**

- **Activity:**
- Participants engage in role-playing exercises where they must adopt positions that oppose the majority view within their teams. Facilitators provide scenarios that are typical at OptiTech, encouraging participants to express and justify dissenting opinions.
- **Impact:**
- This exercise helps team members become more comfortable with expressing and handling dissent, reinforcing the value of diverse viewpoints and critical debate.

1. **Debate Sessions:**

- **Activity:**
- Structured debates are set up where teams argue opposing sides of a proposed business strategy or technological solution. Each team is tasked with researching their position and presenting compelling arguments.
- **Impact:**
- Debates foster an environment where critical evaluation is valued over unanimity, helping team members practice how to articulate and defend their views constructively.

1. **Preventative Strategies Workshop:**

- **Activity:**
- A workshop is conducted on specific strategies to prevent groupthink, including appointing a devil's advocate, fostering an open climate for feedback, and conducting regular review sessions where decisions are critically examined.
- **Impact:**
- Participants learn practical tools and organizational strategies that can be implemented to prevent groupthink, enhancing the team's overall decision-making capacity.

Elena closes the session by facilitating a group reflection on the importance of maintaining vigilance against groupthink. She encourages ongoing personal responsibility to foster a culture where questioning and critical thinking are seen as assets.

The team leaves the workshop with a strong understanding of the dangers of groupthink and equipped with strategies to foster a more open, critically engaging, and innovative workplace.

As the team disperses, there's a noticeable shift in their interactions—more questioning, more discussions, and a palpable respect for diverse perspectives. Elena watches with satisfaction, knowing that by addressing and mitigating groupthink, OptiTech is set to become a stronger, more resilient company.

Virtual Teams and Managing Remote Workers

With a new understanding of the dangers of groupthink, Elena turns her focus to a modern challenge in the world of team dynamics: managing virtual teams and remote workers. As OptiTech's workforce becomes increasingly global, Elena sets up a "Virtual Team Success Workshop" in OptiTech's main conference hall, which is equipped with state-of-the-art communication and collaboration technologies simulating a fully remote working environment.

The OptiTech team members arrive at the conference hall to find it transformed into a high-tech hub with stations representing different global locations. Screens display live feeds from OptiTech's international offices, and workstations are set up to mimic home offices, creating an immersive remote work experience. Elena, aware of the unique challenges and opportunities presented by virtual teamwork, prepares to guide her team through effective strategies for managing remote workers.

Elena begins the workshop with an overview of the evolving workplace landscape, highlighting the rise of remote work and its implications for team cohesion and productivity. She discusses the importance of adapting management styles to effectively lead dispersed teams and introduces the concepts and tools that will be explored during the workshop.

Interactive Activities:

1. **Remote Collaboration Simulation:**

    - **Activity:**

- Teams are divided into groups and assigned to different "offices" around the hall. They are tasked with completing a project using only digital communication tools, such as video conferencing, shared documents, and real-time collaboration platforms.
- **Impact:**
- This simulation provides hands-on experience with remote work challenges, such as time zone differences and communication delays, teaching teams how to stay connected and productive.

1. **Cultural Competence Training:**

- **Activity:**
- A cultural expert conducts a session on global communication styles, sensitivities, and strategies for overcoming cultural barriers within virtual teams.
- **Impact:**
- This training enhances understanding and respect for cultural differences, which is critical for the success of multinational remote teams.

1. **Leadership in Virtual Settings Workshop:**

- **Activity:**
- A leadership coach presents techniques for effectively managing and motivating remote workers, including setting clear expectations, using technology to create a sense of presence, and maintaining regular check-ins.
- **Impact:**
- Leaders learn how to adapt their management techniques

to support transparency, autonomy, and engagement in a virtual environment.

1. **Well-being and Connectivity Session:**

- **Activity:**
- Discussions and activities focus on the well-being of remote workers, exploring how to build a supportive community remotely and how to recognize signs of burnout or disengagement without face-to-face interactions.
- **Impact:**
- Promotes strategies for maintaining mental health and emotional connection, ensuring remote team members feel valued and integrated.

At the close of the workshop, Elena brings everyone together to reflect on the learning experiences and gather feedback on the simulation exercises. She emphasizes the importance of continuous learning and adaptation as OptiTech expands its remote workforce.

The team leaves the workshop with a greater appreciation of the complexities of remote team management and equipped with the tools and knowledge to build thriving virtual teams.

As Elena watches her team engage enthusiastically with the new tools and strategies, she feels confident that OptiTech is well-prepared to face the challenges of a global, digital-first workplace. The workshop has not only equipped the team with necessary skills but also fostered a sense of unity and purpose, crucial for navigating the future of work.

Building High-Performance Teams

Encouraged by the success of the Virtual Team Success Workshop, Elena decides to focus on the ultimate goal of all her efforts: building high-performance teams that not only excel in their tasks but also embody OptiTech's values and vision. She transforms a large, open area of the office into a dynamic workshop space, equipped with various stations designed to emphasize aspects like productivity, innovation, communication, and resilience.

The OptiTech team gathers in the newly arranged space, intrigued by the series of high-energy, collaborative challenges that await them. Elena, understanding that high-performance teams are more than the sum of their parts, prepares a day filled with activities that combine both skill enhancement and team synergy development.

With the entire team assembled, Elena introduces the day with an inspiring talk about what makes a team high-performing. She outlines key characteristics such as deep trust, unwavering commitment, clear goals, effective communication, and the ability to navigate through conflicts constructively. She stresses the importance of adaptability and continuous improvement, setting the stage for a transformative day.

Interactive Activities:

1. **Performance Challenges:**

   - **Activity:**
   - Teams compete in a series of timed challenges that

simulate typical project scenarios but require extraordinary teamwork, strategic planning, and execution under pressure. These include puzzle-solving, product pitching, and rapid prototyping under time constraints.
- **Impact:**
- These challenges push teams to perform at their highest level, emphasizing the importance of leveraging each member's strengths and working cohesively under pressure.

1. **Innovation Tournaments:**

- **Activity:**
- Teams are given a set of tools and a broad problem statement related to OptiTech's market. They must innovate a product or solution that aligns with the company's goals. The best ideas are pitched to a panel of judges.
- **Impact:**
- This tournament fosters creativity and rapid innovation, crucial traits of high-performance teams, while also highlighting the necessity of aligning with the strategic direction of the company.

1. **Resilience Workshops:**

- **Activity:**
- A psychologist leads workshops on resilience, teaching strategies for coping with setbacks, stress, and failure. Role-playing and group discussions help embed these strategies.

- **Impact:**
- Equipping teams with resilience skills ensures they can maintain performance levels even under adverse conditions, a key attribute of successful teams.

1. **Feedback and Reflection Roundtables:**

- **Activity:**
- Teams engage in structured feedback sessions where they provide constructive feedback to each other based on the day's activities. Facilitators guide the teams on how to give and receive feedback effectively.
- **Impact:**
- This activity reinforces the role of continuous feedback in driving improvement and sustaining high performance within teams.

As the day winds down, Elena gathers all the participants to reflect on their experiences and discuss how the lessons learned can be translated into their daily work routines. She emphasizes the journey of becoming a high-performance team as ongoing, with each day offering new opportunities for growth.

The team leaves the workshop feeling empowered and more connected. They have practical tools and insights into what they can achieve together when they truly function as a high-performance team.

Watching her team, now buzzing with new ideas and a renewed sense of camaraderie, Elena feels confident that these efforts will translate into tangible improvements in how teams operate at OptiTech. She knows that today's exercises have laid a stronger foundation for team performance that will drive the company's success in the competitive tech industry.

6

Chapter 6: Leadership in Organizations

Following the successful workshop on building high-performance teams, Elena recognizes the need to focus specifically on enhancing leadership skills within OptiTech. To address this, she organizes a "Leadership Excellence Retreat" at a luxurious mountain resort, offering a serene environment conducive to reflection, learning, and growth. The retreat is designed to redefine leadership within the company, emphasizing adaptability, innovation, and empathy.

As the OptiTech team arrives at the resort, surrounded by panoramic mountain views and lush greenery, the setting immediately instills a sense of peace and possibility. Elena, aware that the success of her organization hinges on the quality of its leaders, has prepared a comprehensive program that includes seminars, interactive workshops, and outdoor leadership challenges.

Elena opens the retreat by discussing the evolving nature of leadership in the digital age. She highlights the importance of leaders who can inspire and guide their teams through rapid technological changes and global challenges. She sets the tone for the retreat by encouraging openness to new ideas and commitment to personal and professional growth.

Interactive Activities:

1. **Leadership Theory Seminars:**

- **Activity:**
- Experts in leadership theories provide seminars on various styles, including transformational, servant, and situational leadership. Each seminar includes case studies of renowned leaders who embody these styles.
- **Impact:**
- These sessions provide theoretical underpinnings and real-world applications, allowing participants to visualize how different styles can be effective in various scenarios at OptiTech.

1. **Self-Assessment and Reflection:**

- **Activity:**
- Leaders engage in guided self-assessment exercises to identify their strengths and areas for improvement. Facilitated reflection sessions help them understand how their personal leadership style impacts their team's dynamics and performance.
- **Impact:**
- This introspective activity encourages leaders to critically evaluate their own leadership approaches and plan for

deliberate development in areas of weakness.

1. **Outdoor Leadership Challenges:**

- **Activity:**
- Participants tackle physical and strategic challenges in the resort's adventure park, designed to simulate workplace scenarios that require leadership under pressure.
- **Impact:**
- These challenges foster teamwork and resilience, pushing leaders to practice decision-making, communication, and resource management in high-pressure, real-time environments.

1. **Innovative Leadership Workshops:**

- **Activity:**
- Interactive workshops focus on innovative leadership practices, such as leading remote teams, integrating AI in management, and fostering a culture of innovation.
- **Impact:**
- Leaders learn to harness technology and creativity to drive their teams forward, ensuring that OptiTech remains at the cutting edge of the tech industry.

1. **Empathy and Emotional Intelligence Training:**

- **Activity:**
- A professional psychologist conducts workshops on developing empathy and emotional intelligence, emphasizing their importance in modern leadership.

- **Impact:**
- By enhancing their emotional intelligence, leaders at OptiTech can better connect with, motivate, and support their teams, leading to improved employee satisfaction and loyalty.

As the retreat concludes, Elena gathers everyone for a final evening by a bonfire. She invites reflections on the retreat and commitments to apply learned skills back at the workplace. Elena emphasizes the continuous journey of leadership development and the role each leader plays in shaping the future of OptiTech.

The leaders leave the retreat with renewed energy, enhanced skills, and a deeper understanding of their role in navigating the complexities of the modern workplace. They are ready to implement innovative leadership strategies that will drive OptiTech's success.

As the flames of the bonfire flicker against the night sky, Elena looks on at her team of leaders, feeling confident and inspired. She knows that the insights and bonds formed during this retreat will empower these leaders to guide OptiTech towards a future filled with promise and innovation.

Leadership Theories and Styles

Building on the successful Leadership Excellence Retreat, Elena feels it's crucial to dive deeper into specific leadership theories and styles to further enhance leadership capabilities within OptiTech. She organizes a specialized workshop series back at the headquarters, designed to explore and critically analyze various leadership theories in detail. The sessions are set in OptiTech's state-of-the-art training room, converted into thematic areas for each leadership style discussed.

As OptiTech's leaders gather in the newly designed training room, they find themselves surrounded by distinct zones—each representing a different leadership theory like transformational, transactional, servant, and situational leadership. Elena, determined to equip her leaders with a broad and deep understanding of various styles, has prepared an engaging and educational series of activities.

Elena's Introductory Overview: Elena opens the series with an energetic overview of the significance of understanding diverse leadership theories. She stresses that the more tools a leader has at their disposal, the better they can adapt to different situations and team needs. Elena introduces the first theory of the day, setting the stage for a session of exploration and active learning.

Interactive Activities:

1. **Transformational Leadership Seminar:**

- **Activity:**
- A renowned expert in transformational leadership conducts a seminar explaining the core principles of this style—vision, inspiration, challenge, and support. Leaders participate in group exercises to identify opportunities within their teams to apply these principles.
- **Impact:**
- This seminar helps leaders understand how to inspire and motivate their teams, fostering an environment that encourages innovation and change.

CHAPTER 6: LEADERSHIP IN ORGANIZATIONS

1. **Transactional Leadership Workshop:**

- **Activity:**
- Through interactive workshops, leaders explore the transactional leadership model, focused on clear structures, rewards, and penalties. They engage in role-playing to practice setting specific, measurable, and achievable goals for their teams.
- **Impact:**
- Leaders learn to effectively use rewards and corrective actions to manage team performance, understanding when this style is most effective.

1. **Servant Leadership Roundtable Discussions:**

- **Activity:**
- In roundtable discussions, leaders delve into servant leadership, emphasizing empathy, listening, and community building. Each leader reflects on how to incorporate these elements into their daily leadership practice.
- **Impact:**
- These discussions highlight the importance of prioritizing team members' growth and well-being, enhancing team loyalty and satisfaction.

1. **Situational Leadership Case Studies:**

- **Activity:**
- Leaders analyze case studies that illustrate the situational leadership theory, identifying how to adapt their leadership style based on team maturity and task complexity.

- **Impact:**
- By understanding situational leadership, leaders at OptiTech can more effectively assess and respond to their team's needs in different contexts.

At the end of the series, Elena brings everyone together to reflect on what they've learned about each leadership theory. She encourages an open discussion about integrating these styles into their leadership repertoire, based on both personal and team requirements.

The leaders leave the workshop series with a richer understanding of various leadership theories and practical insights on when and how to apply them. They feel better equipped to lead their teams in a manner that not only drives performance but also fosters a positive, adaptive, and collaborative work environment.

As the sessions conclude, Elena observes the animated discussions among her leaders, pleased with their enthusiasm and engagement. She is confident that the diverse leadership styles explored will enhance the adaptability and effectiveness of OptiTech's leadership, ensuring the company's continued growth and success in the competitive tech industry.

The Distinction Between Leadership and Management

After delving into various leadership theories and styles, Elena decides it's crucial to clarify the often-misunderstood distinction between leadership and management for the OptiTech team. To address this, she sets up a day-long symposium in OptiTech's largest conference room, themed as a "Leadership vs. Management" exploration lab, complete with discussion zones, interactive digital displays, and role-playing areas.

As OptiTech's team leaders and managers assemble in the conference room, they find themselves surrounded by a setting designed to dissect and analyze the roles of leaders versus managers through practical examples and engaging activities. Elena, aware of the potential for growth that understanding these roles offers, prepares to guide her team through a series of insightful exercises.

Elena starts the symposium by emphasizing the critical roles both leaders and managers play in the success of OptiTech. She outlines the fundamental differences between leadership, which she frames as the art of motivating a group towards achieving a common vision, and management, which involves the careful organization and coordination of tasks to achieve corporate goals.

Interactive Activities:

1. **Interactive Digital Presentations:**

- **Activity:**
- Participants move through interactive digital stations that explain key aspects of leadership and management. Each station is equipped with videos, quizzes, and real-life case studies that illustrate how these roles manifest in a corporate setting.
- **Impact:**
- These presentations help clarify the conceptual differences by providing clear, contextual examples that delineate the visionary role of leaders from the operational role of managers.

1. **Role-Playing Scenarios:**

- **Activity:**
- In the role-playing zone, participants assume the roles of either a leader or a manager in various scenarios such as guiding a team through change (leadership) versus organizing a team to meet project deadlines (management).
- **Impact:**
- Acting out these roles helps participants experience firsthand the practical differences in approach and mindset required for each role, enhancing their understanding and empathy for both functions.

1. **Group Discussions and Debates:**

- **Activity:**
- Facilitated group discussions and debates are organized to delve deeper into the importance of both roles. Participants debate scenarios where leadership was more crucial than management and vice versa, discussing the outcomes and what could have been improved.
- **Impact:**
- These discussions foster a deeper understanding of when and how to apply leadership and management skills effectively, recognizing that both are necessary for different aspects of team and project success.

1. **Expert Panel Q&A:**

- **Activity:**
- A panel of industry leaders and experienced managers is

invited to share their insights on balancing leadership and management responsibilities. The Q&A session allows participants to ask questions directly related to their experiences and challenges at OptiTech.
- **Impact:**
- Hearing from experienced professionals provides real-world advice and strategies for navigating the complex interplay between leading and managing, reinforcing the day's learning.

At the close of the symposium, Elena brings everyone together to summarize the day's insights. She encourages her team to reflect on their roles and consider how they can integrate both leadership and management competencies to enhance their effectiveness.

The team leaves the symposium with a clearer distinction between leadership and management roles, equipped with strategies to balance these effectively within their roles at OptiTech.

As the participants leave the conference room, their discussions echoing in the hall, Elena feels a profound sense of achievement. She knows that by clarifying these roles, she has empowered her team to navigate their responsibilities more effectively, fostering a work environment that is both visionary and well-organized. This understanding is crucial for OptiTech's continued growth and success in the ever-evolving tech landscape.

The Role of a Leader in Shaping Organizational Culture

Following the enlightening symposium on leadership versus management, Elena focuses on another pivotal aspect of leadership—the role of leaders in shaping organizational culture. To explore this in depth, she arranges a unique "Cultural Shaping Retreat" at a serene coastal retreat center, designed to allow leaders to reflect on and actively engage with the elements of culture they wish to cultivate at OptiTech.

As the OptiTech leadership team arrives at the breezy, sunlit retreat center overlooking the ocean, they are met with an atmosphere of introspection and possibility. Elena, knowing that the tone and values of an organization are often a reflection of its leadership, has prepared a series of workshops and activities focused on identifying, understanding, and influencing the cultural dynamics within OptiTech.

Elena begins the retreat with a heartfelt talk on the importance of organizational culture in driving employee engagement, satisfaction, and performance. She explains that leaders are not just administrators but also culture champions, tasked with embodying and promoting the values that make OptiTech unique and successful.

Interactive Activities:

1. **Vision and Values Workshop:**

   - **Activity:**
   - Leaders participate in a workshop to revisit and potentially redefine OptiTech's core values and vision. They

work in groups to discuss how these values are currently manifested in the organization and brainstorm ways to more effectively integrate them into daily operations.
- **Impact:**
- This workshop helps leaders align on a coherent set of core values and a shared vision, which are essential for a unified and effective organizational culture.

1. **Role-Modeling Scenarios:**

- **Activity:**
- In role-playing scenarios, leaders practice situations where they must model positive behaviors and make decisions that reflect organizational values, especially during challenging times.
- **Impact:**
- These scenarios reinforce the importance of leaders as role models, demonstrating the impact of their behavior on the organization's culture and the behavior of their teams.

1. **Cultural Storytelling Sessions:**

- **Activity:**
- Leaders share stories of moments when OptiTech's culture was particularly evident in achieving success or overcoming obstacles. These stories are recorded and discussed for potential use in onboarding new employees.
- **Impact:**
- Storytelling serves as a powerful tool for reinforcing cultural values and helping leaders see the tangible benefits

of a strong organizational culture.

1. **Feedback and Adaptation Circles:**

- **Activity:**
- Small groups form feedback circles where leaders can share and receive input on their effectiveness in promoting and adhering to the company's values in their management practices.
- **Impact:**
- These feedback sessions provide leaders with critical insights into how they are perceived and offer opportunities for personal and professional growth in their roles as culture shapers.

At the end of the retreat, Elena gathers everyone for a closing session by the shoreline at sunset. She encourages leaders to commit to specific actions they will take to foster and reinforce OptiTech's culture. She stresses the continuous nature of this process and the need for constant vigilance and effort to maintain and evolve the company's culture positively.

The leaders leave the retreat with a renewed commitment to actively shape and influence OptiTech's culture. They are equipped with practical tools and strategies to ensure that the organizational culture remains a driving force for innovation, engagement, and competitive advantage.

As the retreat concludes and leaders depart, their thoughtful conversations and resolved expressions reflect their readiness to embrace their roles as culture champions. Elena watches them, feeling confident that her leadership team is now better prepared to steer OptiTech toward a future where the company culture is not only maintained but celebrated and enhanced through their actions.

Transformational vs. Transactional Leadership

With a renewed focus on leadership's role in shaping organizational culture, Elena decides to delve deeper into specific leadership styles that could influence OptiTech's future. She organizes a leadership style showdown at OptiTech's headquarters, setting up two contrasting zones in the main conference hall: one for transformational leadership and one for transactional leadership. Each zone is equipped with case studies, role-playing activities, and technology to simulate real-life scenarios, allowing leaders to experience the nuances and impacts of each style.

As the OptiTech leaders enter the conference hall, they find it divided into two distinct realms. Each zone represents a world governed by different leadership principles: the transformational zone radiates with images of vision and change, while the transactional zone is structured around order and clarity. Elena, aiming to provide her leaders with a comprehensive understanding of these styles, prepares to guide them through a series of exercises designed to highlight the strengths and limitations of each approach.

Elena starts the session by explaining the fundamental differences between transformational and transactional leadership styles. She discusses how transformational leaders inspire and motivate employees to change expectations, perceptions, and motivations to work towards common goals, whereas transactional leaders focus on the exchange that occurs between leaders and followers, emphasizing orderly structure and clear rewards for specific tasks.

Interactive Activities:

1. **Transformational Leadership Workshops:**

- **Activity:**
- Leaders engage in workshops where they learn to develop and communicate a compelling vision, foster an environment that encourages innovation, and support personal development of their team members. The workshops include creating inspirational speeches and simulating crisis situations where they must motivate their teams.
- **Impact:**
- This helps leaders experience the power of transformational leadership to elevate employee morale and drive significant change within the organization.

1. **Transactional Leadership Simulations:**

- **Activity:**
- In this zone, leaders participate in simulations that emphasize setting clear goals, using reward systems effectively, and maintaining strict organizational standards. Scenarios include budget management, project delivery under tight deadlines, and performance evaluations based on precise metrics.
- **Impact:**
- Leaders learn to apply transactional techniques to efficiently manage and motivate teams to achieve specific results, understanding when this approach is most bene-

ficial.

1. **Debate Forum:**

- **Activity:**
- A debate is set up where leaders argue which style is more effective for OptiTech, considering its current challenges and strategic goals. Each leader presents arguments based on scenarios experienced in the workshops and simulations.
- **Impact:**
- This activity fosters a deeper understanding of the applicability of each leadership style, highlighting that the best approach may often involve a blend of both styles depending on the situation.

1. **Feedback and Reflection Session:**

- **Activity:**
- Leaders gather to discuss their experiences and provide feedback on the exercises. This session includes reflective questions to help leaders consider how their preferred style affects their decision-making and team interactions.
- **Impact:**
- Encourages self-awareness among leaders about their natural leadership tendencies and the potential need to adapt their style to better meet the needs of their teams and organizational goals.

As the day concludes, Elena brings everyone together to summarize the insights gained from exploring both leadership styles. She emphasizes the importance of flexibility in leadership approaches and encourages her leaders to think critically about how they can integrate the best aspects of both styles into their leadership repertoire.

The leaders leave the session with a nuanced understanding of transformational and transactional leadership, equipped with practical skills and insights into when and how to apply each style to enhance team performance and organizational success.

As the leaders file out of the conference hall, there's a buzz of animated discussion about the day's learning experiences. Elena watches them, satisfied with the depth of engagement and confident that this exploration has equipped her leaders with the tools to navigate the complexities of modern leadership at OptiTech.

Contemporary Leadership Challenges (e.g., Leading Millennials)

With the insightful exploration of transformational and transactional leadership styles still resonating, Elena decides to address a pressing contemporary issue that affects many organizations globally: leading millennials. Recognizing that generational differences can significantly impact leadership effectiveness, she organizes a "Generational Leadership Workshop" at OptiTech's innovation hub. The venue is set up with modern, casual seating arrangements, tech-savvy presentation tools, and breakout rooms for interactive sessions.

As the OptiTech leaders gather in the innovation hub, they find themselves immersed in a workshop designed to bridge generational gaps and foster understanding. The space buzzes with anticipation as participants from various generations prepare to explore the unique challenges and opportunities of leading millennials, who are known for their distinct values and work preferences. Elena, committed to equipping her leaders with the skills to manage a diverse workforce effectively, prepares to guide them through a series of tailored activities.

Elena starts the workshop by discussing the importance of adaptability in leadership, particularly in the context of a multigenerational workplace. She highlights the characteristics commonly attributed to millennials—such as their need for purpose, preference for flexible work conditions, and their adeptness with technology—and explains how these traits require a nuanced approach to leadership.

Interactive Activities:

1. **Understanding Millennials Seminar:**

- **Activity:**
- A guest speaker who specializes in generational studies provides an in-depth look at what motivates millennials at work, including their values, communication styles, and career expectations.
- **Impact:**
- This session helps leaders understand the underlying factors that influence millennial behaviors and attitudes, enabling them to tailor their leadership strategies to better engage with this cohort.

1. **Role-Playing Leadership Scenarios:**

- **Activity:**
- Leaders engage in role-playing exercises that involve managing hypothetical situations involving millennial employees, such as negotiating work arrangements, addressing feedback preferences, and leveraging technology for productivity.
- **Impact:**
- These scenarios allow leaders to practice and refine their approaches to common challenges faced when leading millennials, enhancing their interpersonal and management skills.

1. **Panel Discussion: Insights from Millennial Leaders:**

- **Activity:**
- A panel of successful millennial leaders from various industries shares insights and experiences about what leadership styles and practices have most effectively motivated them.
- **Impact:**
- Hearing directly from millennials provides valuable perspectives and allows senior leaders to question assumptions and update their leadership tactics.

1. **Collaborative Strategy Development:**

- **Activity:**
- Leaders collaborate in groups to develop actionable strategies that incorporate the workshop learnings to

improve leadership across generational divides within their teams at OptiTech.
- **Impact:**
- This collaborative session fosters a sense of community and shared responsibility among leaders to proactively address generational challenges and harness the potential of a diverse workforce.

As the workshop concludes, Elena gathers all participants for a closing reflection. She encourages them to continue exploring and adapting to the needs of different generations. She emphasizes that effective leadership in a contemporary setting is dynamic and constantly evolving.

The leaders leave the workshop equipped with a deeper understanding of millennial characteristics, motivations, and needs. They feel more confident in their ability to lead such a diverse group effectively, ensuring that OptiTech remains a vibrant and inclusive place to work.

As the leaders disperse, their animated discussions reflect a renewed commitment to embracing generational diversity. Elena watches with satisfaction, knowing that these efforts will lead to a more harmonious and productive workplace, ready to meet the challenges of the future with a well-led, motivated team.

7

Chapter 7: Decision Making

Following the leadership workshops, Elena recognizes a pivotal area that often challenges even the most seasoned leaders: decision making. To equip her team with advanced decision-making skills, she organizes a "Decision-Making Mastery Retreat" at a remote and serene lakeside resort. This tranquil environment is ideal for deep thinking and strategic planning, equipped with conference rooms for seminars and outdoor spaces for reflective solo and group activities.

As the leaders of OptiTech arrive at the serene retreat, they are surrounded by the peaceful, natural beauty of the lakeside, creating a perfect backdrop for clear thinking and focus. The retreat is designed to explore various decision-making processes and techniques, encouraging leaders to engage in both theoretical learning and practical application.

With the gentle sound of the lake's waves in the background, Elena begins the retreat by discussing the critical role of decision making in leadership. She stresses that effective decision-making can significantly influence the success and direction of the entire organization. She introduces the key themes for the retreat: types of decision-making processes, the role of data and intuition, and strategies to avoid common pitfalls like analysis paralysis and decision fatigue.

Interactive Activities:

1. **Workshop on Decision-Making Models:**

- **Activity:**
- A series of workshops led by decision-making experts who introduce various models such as rational decision making, the bounded rationality model, and intuitive decision making. Each workshop includes case studies that require leaders to apply these models to hypothetical business scenarios.
- **Impact:**
- Leaders learn to identify which decision-making models are best suited to different types of decisions, enhancing their ability to choose appropriate strategies based on the context.

1. **Data vs. Intuition Debate:**

- **Activity:**
- A structured debate on the merits and limitations of data-driven versus intuition-based decision making. Leaders are divided into teams and given roles to argue from both perspectives, backed by real-world examples and research.
- **Impact:**

- This activity helps leaders understand the balance between leveraging vast amounts of data available in today's digital world and relying on personal and collective intuition.

1. **Crisis Simulation Exercise:**

- **Activity:**
- Leaders participate in a real-time crisis simulation that challenges them to make quick decisions under pressure. The simulation includes unexpected twists and complex variables that mimic real-world crises.
- **Impact:**
- This exercise tests leaders' abilities to maintain composure, think critically, and make decisions swiftly during high-pressure situations.

1. **Solo Reflection Walks:**

- **Activity:**
- Leaders are encouraged to take solo walks along the lakeside, provided with reflective questions about their decision-making styles and past decisions. This quiet time allows for introspection about personal strengths and areas for improvement.
- **Impact:**
- Solo walks provide leaders with the opportunity to introspect deeply about their decision-making process and the personal biases that might affect their judgments.

As the sun sets over the lake on the final day of the retreat,

Elena gathers everyone for a fireside chat. She invites leaders to share their insights and commitments to apply what they've learned about decision making to enhance their leadership back at OptiTech.

The leaders leave the retreat with enhanced decision-making skills, a deeper understanding of various decision-making processes, and practical experiences that will help them navigate complex business landscapes effectively.

Watching her team prepare to depart, Elena feels a profound sense of accomplishment. She is confident that the decision-making skills honed here will significantly impact OptiTech's future success, guiding the team through uncertainties with wisdom and clarity.

Types of Organizational Decisions

After concluding the impactful Decision-Making Mastery Retreat, Elena plans to extend the learning journey back at OptiTech's headquarters. She designs a series of workshops specifically tailored to explore the different types of organizational decisions leaders face daily. The workshop series, titled "Decision Landscapes," is held in a large, multi-functional space at the office, transformed into various decision-making stations, each representing a different type of decision.

As OptiTech leaders gather in the newly designed workshop space, they find themselves surrounded by zones labeled as "Strategic Decisions," "Tactical Decisions," "Operational Decisions," and "Crisis Decisions." Each area is equipped with interactive tools and case studies, reflecting the complexities and impacts of these decision types. Elena, intent on deepening the leaders' understanding and enhancing their decision-making agility, prepares to guide them through a day of intensive learning and application.

Elena starts the workshop with an overview of the spectrum of decision-making types within an organization. She highlights how each type requires different approaches and considerations, affecting the company's short-term actions and long-term strategy. She encourages the leaders to engage deeply with the exercises, noting that mastery of diverse decision-making will significantly enhance their leadership effectiveness.

Interactive Activities:

1. **Strategic Decisions Zone:**

- **Activity:**
- Leaders engage in scenario-based simulations that involve making high-level strategic decisions such as entering new markets, investing in R&D for new technologies, or changing organizational structure.
- **Impact:**
- This zone helps leaders understand the implications of strategic decisions on the organization's future, emphasizing the need for vision and forward-thinking.

1. **Tactical Decisions Workshop:**

- **Activity:**
- This workshop focuses on tactical decisions such as resource allocation, sales targets, and marketing strategies. Leaders use interactive dashboards to analyze data and

make decisions that align with the company's strategic goals.
- **Impact:**
- Leaders learn to bridge the gap between strategic plans and operational actions, enhancing their ability to execute strategies effectively.

1. **Operational Decisions Station:**

- **Activity:**
- At this station, leaders handle day-to-day decision-making scenarios that affect the company's operations, such as scheduling, quality control, and customer service responses.
- **Impact:**
- This hands-on approach reinforces the importance of operational decisions in maintaining efficient, high-quality business processes.

1. **Crisis Decisions Simulation:**

- **Activity:**
- Leaders are thrust into a real-time crisis simulation where they must make quick, impactful decisions to navigate hypothetical scenarios such as cybersecurity attacks or public relations crises.
- **Impact:**
- Simulating crisis situations tests leaders' abilities to think and act under pressure, emphasizing the skills necessary to manage unexpected challenges effectively.

At the end of the day, Elena gathers the leaders for a debriefing session in which they reflect on their experiences across different decision-making types. She encourages them to share insights and discuss how they can apply what they've learned to their roles.

The leaders leave the workshop with a deeper understanding of the diverse types of decisions they will encounter and the strategies required to address them effectively. They appreciate the nuances of each decision type and feel better equipped to lead their teams through the decision-making processes.

As the workshop concludes and leaders begin to leave, their thoughtful expressions and engaged discussions reflect a readiness to tackle the complexities of their roles with enhanced decision-making skills. Elena watches them, confident that this deep dive into organizational decision types will significantly improve the leadership acumen within OptiTech.

Rational Decision-Making Process

After exploring the various types of organizational decisions, Elena recognizes the need for her team to master a structured approach to decision making. To facilitate this, she organizes a specialized workshop titled "Mastering the Rational Decision-Making Process" in OptiTech's main training center. The center is equipped with decision-making models, flowcharts, and digital tools designed to simulate complex decision scenarios.

As the OptiTech leaders gather in the training center, they are met with a clinical, yet inviting setup that emphasizes clarity and precision—key aspects of the rational decision-making process. Elena, determined to enhance their systematic decision-making skills, has planned a day filled with practical exercises, role-plays, and case studies.

Elena opens the session by explaining the importance of the rational decision-making process, a methodical approach that helps minimize errors and biases in making choices. She outlines the key steps of the process: defining the problem, identifying decision criteria, weighing the criteria, generating alternatives, evaluating the alternatives, choosing the best alternative, and implementing and monitoring the decision.

Interactive Activities:

1. **Problem Definition Exercise:**

- **Activity:**
- Leaders participate in a group exercise to practice defining problems clearly and specifically. They are given vague scenarios common in business settings and tasked with refining these scenarios into well-defined problems.
- **Impact:**
- This exercise emphasizes the importance of accurately identifying and defining problems as the foundation for effective decision-making.

1. **Criteria Weighing Workshop:**

- **Activity:**
- In this session, leaders learn how to identify and assign weights to various decision criteria based on their impor-

tance to the overall goal. Interactive tools allow leaders to manipulate criteria weights and see how different weightings affect the decision outcome.
- **Impact:**
- Leaders gain insights into the critical role of prioritizing decision criteria and how this impacts the outcomes of their decisions.

1. **Alternative Generation and Evaluation Role-Play:**

- **Activity:**
- Leaders role-play scenarios where they must generate and then evaluate different solutions to a business problem using structured evaluation techniques taught during the workshop.
- **Impact:**
- This activity demonstrates the importance of creativity in generating alternatives and the need for a systematic approach to evaluate each alternative's viability.

1. **Decision Implementation Simulation:**

- **Activity:**
- A simulation is set up where leaders choose the best alternative and plan the implementation. They must consider factors like resource allocation, timeline, and potential resistance.
- **Impact:**
- Leaders practice how to effectively implement decisions and monitor their outcomes, understanding that the decision-making process extends beyond just making

a choice.

At the close of the workshop, Elena facilitates a discussion where leaders share their experiences and learnings from the day. She stresses the value of the rational decision-making process in bringing systematic and unbiased judgment to complex business decisions.

The leaders leave the workshop with a comprehensive understanding of the rational decision-making process, equipped with practical tools and strategies to apply this structured approach in their daily work.

As the leaders exit the training center, their discussions buzz with the possibilities of applying rational decision-making techniques. Elena watches on, satisfied that they are now better equipped to face the complexities of their roles, making more informed and effective decisions that will guide OptiTech's path forward.

Common Biases in Decision-Making

Building on the principles of rational decision-making, Elena decides it's critical to address the psychological underpinnings that can undermine it: cognitive biases. To tackle this, she sets up a "Bias Busters Workshop" in OptiTech's main auditorium, transformed into a space resembling a blend of a classroom and an interactive lab, with stations dedicated to different types of biases like confirmation bias, anchoring bias, and groupthink.

As the OptiTech leaders file into the auditorium, they are greeted by a series of interactive installations and stations, each illustrating a specific decision-making bias. Elena, knowing how these unseen cognitive forces can skew even the most rational processes, has designed the workshop to make her team aware of these biases and to teach them strategies to mitigate their effects.

Elena begins by discussing the subtle yet profound impact that cognitive biases can have on decision-making. She explains that while biases are a natural part of human cognition, recognizing and addressing them is crucial for making objective decisions that truly benefit the organization.

Interactive Activities:

1. **Bias Identification Challenge:**

- **Activity:**
- Leaders rotate through stations, each simulating decision-making scenarios that subtly incorporate different biases. Participants must identify the bias at play and discuss its potential impact on the decision outcome.
- **Impact:**
- This challenge helps leaders become more aware of their own susceptibility to biases, a critical first step in managing them effectively.

1. **Workshop on Mitigating Biases:**

- **Activity:**
- A facilitated workshop provides techniques and tools to mitigate biases, such as structured analytic techniques, pre-mortem analysis, and the deliberate consideration of opposing viewpoints.

- **Impact:**
- Leaders learn practical methods to reduce the influence of biases in their decision-making processes, enhancing their ability to lead objectively.

1. **Role-Playing for Perspective-Taking:**

- **Activity:**
- Leaders engage in role-playing exercises where they must argue from perspectives that oppose their initial opinions. This activity is designed to combat confirmation bias and open leaders up to a broader range of viewpoints.
- **Impact:**
- By experiencing the validity of alternative viewpoints, leaders can better appreciate the value of diverse opinions in enriching decision-making processes.

1. **Group Decision-Making Simulation:**

- **Activity:**
- In this simulation, groups of leaders must make decisions under time pressure, allowing them to observe how stress and group dynamics can lead to rushed decisions influenced by biases like groupthink.
- **Impact:**
- This exercise highlights the need for maintaining vigilance against biases even—or especially—under pressure.

As the workshop winds down, Elena gathers everyone for a closing session to reflect on what they've learned about biases and how they affect decisions. She encourages an ongoing dialogue about biases in their respective teams and stresses the importance of fostering a culture that values critical thinking and skepticism.

Leaders leave the workshop more mindful of the common biases that can affect their decision-making. They are equipped with new strategies to challenge their assumptions and ensure more balanced, informed decisions within their teams.

Elena watches her team engage in animated discussions as they exit the auditorium, confident that they are now better prepared to recognize and counteract the subtle biases that challenge objective decision-making. This newfound awareness and toolkit will play a crucial role in steering OptiTech towards more thoughtful and effective leadership.

Group Decision-Making Techniques

After a deep dive into common biases that can affect decision-making, Elena feels it's essential to shift focus towards enhancing group decision-making dynamics at OptiTech. To this end, she organizes a "Group Decision Dynamics Workshop" in the company's large collaborative space, which is set up with round tables for team activities, high-tech polling tools for anonymous voting, and areas designated for breakout sessions and group discussions.

As the leaders of OptiTech gather in the collaborative space, they find themselves in a setup that encourages open communication and consensus-building. The room is abuzz with anticipation for a session designed to not only teach effective group decision-making techniques but also to practice them in real-time. Elena, committed to fostering a culture of inclusive and efficient decision-making, prepares to engage the team with a mix of theoretical instruction and practical exercises.

Elena begins by emphasizing the importance of group decisions in leveraging diverse perspectives to achieve better outcomes. She outlines the day's agenda, which includes exploring various group decision-making techniques such as the Delphi method, brainstorming, nominal group technique, and consensus building. She encourages everyone to participate actively and keep an open mind.

Interactive Activities:

1. **Brainstorming Session:**

- **Activity:**
- Leaders participate in a classic brainstorming session aimed at generating creative solutions to a new market challenge facing OptiTech. Facilitators guide the session to ensure that all ideas are heard without immediate judgment or criticism.
- **Impact:**
- This exercise demonstrates how free-flowing creativity can lead to innovative solutions and highlights the importance of suspending judgment to encourage idea generation.

1. **Nominal Group Technique Workshop:**

- **Activity:**
- This workshop introduces leaders to the nominal group

technique where they individually write down ideas, share them round-robin style, discuss and clarify, and then vote privately to rank the options.
- **Impact:**
- The nominal group technique helps minimize the domination of the discussion by a few voices and ensures that all members contribute to the decision-making process, making it more democratic and inclusive.

1. **Delphi Method Simulation:**

- **Activity:**
- Leaders engage in a Delphi method exercise, where they independently answer questionnaires on a strategic decision, followed by discussion and revision based on anonymous summaries of the group's responses.
- **Impact:**
- This activity shows how iterative rounds of discussion and anonymous feedback can converge on a solution that reflects a deep level of group insight and minimizes peer pressure.

1. **Consensus Building Exercise:**

- **Activity:**
- Teams work through a complex scenario requiring a significant strategic decision. They must apply consensus-building techniques to arrive at a decision that accommodates the interests of all group members.
- **Impact:**
- Leaders learn the value of developing agreements that

everyone can support, understanding the process of negotiating and modifying proposals to address the concerns of group members.

Elena closes the workshop by facilitating a reflection session where leaders share their experiences and insights from the day's activities. She highlights the strengths and challenges of each technique and encourages the leaders to think about how they can implement these strategies within their teams.

The leaders leave the workshop equipped with multiple group decision-making techniques, understanding when and how each method can be applied to enhance decision quality and team cohesion.

As the leaders disperse, engaged in thoughtful discussion about their new tools and techniques, Elena feels confident that these enhanced group decision-making skills will lead to more effective and harmonious decision processes at OptiTech, ultimately driving the company toward greater innovation and success.

The Role of AI in Decision Making

Having enriched the OptiTech leadership's understanding of various decision-making techniques, Elena sees an opportunity to integrate modern technology into their decision-making processes. She organizes a cutting-edge workshop titled "AI and Decision Making" at OptiTech's main campus, transforming a large tech lab into an interactive space with stations dedicated to AI-driven analytics, predictive modeling, and real-time decision support systems.

As the leaders of OptiTech arrive at the tech lab, they're

greeted by an array of digital displays and devices demonstrating AI's capabilities in data analysis and prediction. The air buzzes with the potential of technology to transform traditional decision-making. Elena, intent on guiding her team towards a future where human insight and artificial intelligence collaborate seamlessly, prepares to demonstrate the powerful role AI can play in enhancing business decisions.

Elena starts the workshop with an overview of AI's impact on modern business practices, highlighting case studies where AI has significantly improved decision accuracy and efficiency. She explains that today's focus will be on understanding AI's capabilities, exploring its benefits, and discussing its implications for leadership and decision-making at OptiTech.

Interactive Activities:

1. **AI Analytics Demonstration:**

   - **Activity:**
   - Leaders interact with AI systems that analyze large datasets to identify trends and patterns that are difficult for humans to discern. They work through scenarios using AI to make predictive analyses in areas like market trends, customer behavior, and operational efficiency.
   - **Impact:**
   - This demonstration showcases how AI can provide deep insights that inform strategic decisions, reducing guesswork and enhancing data-driven strategies.

1. **Predictive Modeling Workshop:**

- **Activity:**
- A hands-on workshop where leaders use AI tools to create predictive models for various business outcomes, such as sales forecasts or product development successes. They test different variables and assess the AI's accuracy in real-time.
- **Impact:**
- Leaders experience firsthand how AI can be used to simulate potential business scenarios and predict outcomes, helping them to plan more effectively and mitigate risks.

1. **Ethical Decision-Making with AI Roundtable:**

- **Activity:**
- A roundtable discussion facilitated by an AI ethics expert who explores the ethical considerations of using AI in decision making, including bias, transparency, and accountability.
- **Impact:**
- This discussion highlights the ethical dimensions of AI deployment in business, prompting leaders to consider how to use AI responsibly and maintain trust with stakeholders.

1. **Real-Time Decision Support Systems Trial:**

- **Activity:**
- Leaders engage with real-time AI decision support systems that provide immediate data analysis and decision-making recommendations during simulated high-stake meetings.

- **Impact:**
- This trial illustrates how AI can assist in making quicker, more informed decisions in a dynamic business environment, enhancing responsiveness to emerging challenges and opportunities.

At the end of the workshop, Elena gathers the leaders to discuss how AI can be integrated into their decision-making frameworks. She encourages them to consider AI as a tool that complements rather than replaces human judgment, emphasizing the importance of maintaining a strategic balance.

The leaders leave the workshop with a nuanced understanding of how AI can enhance decision-making processes at OptiTech. They recognize the potential for AI to transform their roles, making them more effective as data-driven decision-makers.

As the leaders disperse, energized by the potential of AI-enhanced decision making, Elena reflects on the successful integration of AI into OptiTech's leadership practices. She is confident that this technological empowerment will lead to smarter, faster, and more effective decisions, propelling OptiTech into a future where technology and human insight create unparalleled business solutions.

8

Chapter 8: Power and Politics in Organizations

After successfully integrating AI into decision-making processes at OptiTech, Elena shifts her focus to another critical aspect of organizational dynamics: power and politics. Understanding the complexities and often subtle nature of these elements, she plans an immersive workshop series titled "Navigating Power and Politics." This series is held at OptiTech's main auditorium, now transformed into a simulation center where real-life scenarios involving power dynamics and political maneuvering are enacted.

As the leaders of OptiTech file into the auditorium, they are met with a setting that resembles a large-scale board game. Each station represents different political scenarios ranging from coalition building to conflict resolution and strategic influence. Elena, determined to equip her leaders with the tools to understand and ethically navigate organizational politics, prepares to guide them through understanding the sources of power and the strategies to handle organizational politics effectively.

Elena opens the session by discussing the inevitability of power dynamics and politics in any organization. She emphasizes the importance of recognizing these dynamics not as negative forces but as realities that, when understood and managed properly, can be harnessed to foster positive outcomes for the company.

Interactive Activities:

1. **Power Dynamics Workshop:**

- **Activity:**
- Participants engage in role-playing exercises that illustrate different types of power, such as positional power, expert power, and referent power. Leaders practice scenarios where they must leverage various types of power to influence outcomes and drive initiatives.
- **Impact:**
- This workshop helps leaders recognize different sources of power within themselves and others, enhancing their ability to use power responsibly and effectively.

1. **Political Mapping Session:**

- **Activity:**
- A facilitator guides leaders through the process of creating a "political map" of the organization, identifying key power holders, influencers, and alliances. This activity includes analyzing how these elements interact to affect decision-making and policy implementation.

- **Impact:**
- Leaders learn to identify and understand the political landscape of OptiTech, which is crucial for navigating complex situations and for strategic planning.

1. **Simulation of Organizational Change:**

- **Activity:**
- Leaders participate in a simulated organizational change initiative, requiring them to navigate through resistance, persuade stakeholders, and broker compromises while managing undercurrents of power and politics.
- **Impact:**
- This simulation provides practical experience in managing the political aspects of change, teaching leaders how to secure buy-in and mitigate conflicts.

1. **Ethics in Power and Politics Discussion:**

- **Activity:**
- A moderated discussion focuses on the ethical considerations of using power and engaging in politics within an organization. Topics include the ethical boundaries of influence, the consequences of political maneuvers, and strategies for maintaining integrity.
- **Impact:**
- This discussion reinforces the importance of ethical leadership and helps leaders understand where to draw the line in complex political situations.

As the workshop series concludes, Elena gathers all participants for a final reflection session. She encourages leaders to share their insights and discusses how the understanding of power and politics can be used constructively to advance organizational goals and maintain a healthy workplace culture.

The leaders leave the series with a deeper understanding of the nuanced roles of power and politics in organizational life. They feel better equipped with the skills to navigate these dynamics strategically and ethically.

Watching her team engage in thoughtful discussions as they leave the auditorium, Elena feels confident that they are now better prepared to handle the complexities of power and politics at OptiTech. This awareness and strategic capability are essential for leading effectively in an environment where power dynamics and politics shape much of the organizational landscape.

Definitions of Power and Organizational Politics

To deepen the understanding of power and organizational politics, Elena arranges a seminar series at OptiTech's headquarters, transforming a spacious conference room into a learning hub. The setting is designed for clarity and focus, with multimedia presentations ready to explain theoretical concepts and their practical applications in corporate environments. This series is aimed at demystifying these often-misunderstood aspects of organizational life and providing clear, actionable insights for the leaders.

As OptiTech leaders gather in the conference room, the atmosphere is one of anticipation and curiosity. Elena, intent on providing a solid theoretical foundation before moving into more interactive applications, has organized a day dedicated to understanding the core definitions and frameworks that describe power and politics within organizational contexts.

Elena begins the seminar by emphasizing the critical role of power dynamics and political skills in effective leadership. She introduces the day's agenda, focusing on unpacking the definitions of power and the nature of organizational politics, and how these can be navigated to foster a productive and ethical organizational culture.

Interactive Activities:

1. **Defining Power Presentation:**

- **Activity:**
- A keynote presentation details different types of power identified in scholarly research, including coercive, reward, legitimate, expert, and referent power. Each type of power is illustrated with examples from corporate scenarios, highlighting how they manifest in daily interactions and decision-making processes.
- **Impact:**
- This presentation helps leaders understand and identify the sources of power they and others may wield, setting the stage for more nuanced management of these dynamics.

1. **Organizational Politics Workshop:**

- **Activity:**
- Facilitators lead a workshop where the concept of organizational politics is explored. Discussions focus on

distinguishing negative political behaviors from positive political skills, such as networking, influence, resource allocation, and coalition-building.
- **Impact:**
- By defining what constitutes organizational politics and differentiating harmful behaviors from constructive actions, leaders learn to engage in politics ethically and effectively.

1. **Case Study Breakdown:**

- **Activity:**
- Small groups analyze real-world case studies where power dynamics and political actions played decisive roles in the outcome. Each group presents their analysis, discussing how different forms of power and political tactics were used and what the consequences were.
- **Impact:**
- This activity deepens leaders' understanding of the practical implications of power and politics, providing clearer insights into how these forces can be managed and utilized responsibly.

1. **Role-Playing Political Acumen:**

- **Activity:**
- Leaders engage in role-playing exercises that challenge them to navigate hypothetical yet realistic political scenarios within the company. They practice using political skills to achieve goals without compromising their values or the organizational ethos.

- **Impact:**
- Role-playing helps leaders develop a hands-on understanding of how to apply political skills in ways that are constructive and aligned with OptiTech's ethical standards.

At the close of the seminar, Elena brings everyone together to reflect on the day's learning. She stresses the importance of recognizing and appropriately managing power and politics to lead effectively and maintain a healthy workplace. Elena encourages ongoing education and openness to discussing these topics as part of the leaders' development paths.

The leaders leave the seminar with a comprehensive understanding of power and organizational politics, equipped with the knowledge and tools to navigate these complex dynamics thoughtfully and strategically.

As the participants leave the conference room, their thoughtful discussions and renewed perspectives reflect a readiness to handle the intricacies of power and politics at OptiTech. Elena watches them, satisfied with their progress, knowing that this deeper understanding is crucial for cultivating a leadership team that is not only powerful but also principled and prepared to guide the company forward.

Sources of Power and How It Is Acquired

Inspired by the engagement and insights from the seminar on definitions of power and organizational politics, Elena plans to delve deeper into the sources of power and how leaders can ethically acquire and use it within OptiTech. She sets up a "Power Dynamics Workshop" in the company's innovation lab, equipped with virtual reality setups for simulations, interactive discussion panels, and brainstorming zones, each designed to provide hands-on experience with different aspects of power acquisition and utilization.

As OptiTech's leaders enter the innovation lab, they're greeted by an environment that feels part think tank, part interactive museum. Each station offers a unique exploration of power sources such as positional authority, expert knowledge, and personal influence. Elena, determined to equip her leaders with a deeper understanding of how power can be ethically acquired and wielded to drive positive change, prepares to guide them through a series of activities that highlight the nuances of power dynamics.

Elena opens the workshop with a discussion on the nature of power in organizational settings, emphasizing that power itself is neutral but can have positive or negative impacts based on how it is acquired and used. She outlines the five bases of power identified by social psychologists John French and Bertram Raven: legitimate, reward, coercive, expert, and referent, explaining how each type can play a role in leadership strategies at OptiTech.

Interactive Activities:

1. **Positional Power Simulations:**

- **Activity:**
- Leaders enter virtual reality simulations where they navigate scenarios as senior executives (legitimate power), mid-level managers (reward power), and entry-level positions with limited authority (coercive power seen

from the receiving end). Participants experience the responsibilities and challenges associated with each level of positional power.
- **Impact:**
- This immersive experience helps leaders understand the impact of positional power on decision-making and employee relations, highlighting the importance of using such power responsibly.

1. **Expert and Referent Power Workshops:**

- **Activity:**
- In these workshops, leaders are tasked with solving complex problems using only their knowledge or by influencing others based on their respect and admiration (expert and referent power, respectively). They must convince others of their viewpoints without relying on any formal authority.
- **Impact:**
- Leaders learn to leverage personal capabilities and charisma to influence outcomes, demonstrating how non-positional sources of power can be effective tools in leadership.

1. **Power Acquisition Panel Discussion:**

- **Activity:**
- A panel of seasoned leaders and external experts discuss their experiences in acquiring and using different types of power. They share strategies for developing expert skills, earning respect, and managing the ethical dimensions of

power use.
- **Impact:**
- This discussion provides practical insights and real-world examples that help leaders understand how to develop and acquire power in ways that align with organizational values and ethical standards.

1. **Ethical Power Use Debates:**

- **Activity:**
- Leaders engage in debates over scenarios that pose ethical dilemmas related to the use of power. They explore the boundaries of ethical behavior in exerting influence and the long-term consequences of different approaches.
- **Impact:**
- Debating these scenarios reinforces the critical importance of ethics in power dynamics, encouraging leaders to think deeply about the implications of their actions.

As the workshop concludes, Elena brings everyone together to reflect on their experiences and discuss how the insights gained about power can be integrated into their leadership practices. She emphasizes the importance of continuous learning and ethical considerations when dealing with power dynamics.

The leaders leave the workshop with a nuanced understanding of the different sources of power and how they can be cultivated and applied effectively and ethically within their roles at OptiTech.

As the leaders depart, animated by their new insights and understanding, Elena feels a sense of accomplishment. She is confident that her team is better equipped to handle the complexities of power in leadership, fostering a culture at OptiTech where power is used to motivate, inspire, and achieve collective success.

The Effects of Power on Organizational Behavior

Building on the insightful discussions about the sources of power and its acquisition, Elena recognizes the importance of understanding how power actually influences behavior within the organization. To address this, she sets up an "Influence and Impact" seminar at OptiTech's main auditorium. The seminar is designed to reveal the practical effects of power dynamics on organizational behavior, featuring expert guest speakers, case study presentations, and interactive group simulations.

As OptiTech leaders gather in the auditorium, they find the space transformed into an environment conducive to both learning and reflection. Stations around the room are set up to simulate various organizational scenarios depicting power dynamics. Elena, committed to fostering an environment where power is used constructively and transparently, has meticulously planned a series of activities to illuminate the real effects of power within a corporate setting.

Elena begins the seminar with an overview of how power can subtly or significantly alter behaviors, relationships, and processes within an organization. She explains that understanding these dynamics is crucial for responsible leadership, as the misuse of power can lead to toxic work environments, while its good use can promote innovation and efficiency.

Interactive Activities:

1. **Case Study Analysis:**

- **Activity:**
- Leaders are divided into groups to analyze and present real-world case studies where power dynamics played a pivotal role in shaping organizational outcomes. These case studies include instances of both positive and negative applications of power.
- **Impact:**
- This activity helps leaders see concrete examples of how power can influence organizational behavior, learning from both successes and failures.

1. **Expert Panel Discussions:**

- **Activity:**
- A panel of organizational psychologists and business leaders discuss the psychological effects of power on individuals and teams, including concepts like power corruption, power distance, and empowerment.
- **Impact:**
- These discussions deepen leaders' understanding of the psychological underpinnings of power dynamics, providing them with insights on how to manage these forces ethically and effectively.

1. **Role-Playing Simulations:**

- **Activity:**

- Leaders participate in role-playing exercises where they act out scenarios involving different power structures, such as flat versus hierarchical organizations. They experience firsthand how power levels can affect communication, decision-making, and team morale.
- **Impact:**
- Role-playing allows leaders to experiment with different power dynamics and see the potential impacts on organizational behavior, fostering empathy and strategic thinking.

1. **Group Reflection Sessions:**

- **Activity:**
- Facilitated reflection sessions encourage leaders to think critically about how power is used within their own teams. They discuss strategies to ensure power is exercised responsibly, promoting a culture of accountability and mutual respect.
- **Impact:**
- These sessions help leaders internalize the day's lessons and plan practical applications to enhance their leadership approaches.

As the seminar concludes, Elena gathers all participants for a final reflection. She emphasizes the dual nature of power as both a tool and a test, urging leaders to use their power to foster an inclusive, dynamic, and high-performing organizational culture.

The leaders leave the seminar with a sophisticated understanding of how power affects organizational behavior and a renewed commitment to wielding their influence thoughtfully and constructively.

Watching her team engage in deep discussions as they leave the auditorium, Elena feels confident that they are now better equipped to handle the complexities of power in leadership. She trusts that these insights will guide them to lead OptiTech in a way that maximizes the positive impacts of power while minimizing its potential downsides, ensuring a healthy, productive organizational environment.

Political Tactics and Strategies within Organizations

Following the seminar on the effects of power on organizational behavior, Elena recognizes the need to address the specific tactics and strategies of organizational politics that leaders at OptiTech can encounter and wield effectively. She arranges a detailed workshop titled "Mastering Organizational Politics" in one of the company's executive boardrooms, setting it up to simulate a political battleground where strategic maneuvers, alliances, and power plays are not only demonstrated but also practiced.

As the OptiTech leaders assemble in the boardroom, they find it transformed into various stations that simulate real-life political scenarios, complete with role-playing activities and strategy-building sessions. Elena, understanding that politics can often be seen in a negative light, aims to show how political skills are essential tools for positive influence and organizational success when used ethically and wisely.

Elena begins the workshop by emphasizing that politics is an inherent part of any organizational life and, when understood and applied correctly, can be an asset rather than a hindrance. She outlines the goals of the workshop, which are to identify, understand, and master the political tactics and strategies that leaders can use to navigate and influence their environment effectively.

Interactive Activities:

1. **Political Tactics Training:**

- **Activity:**
- An expert in organizational behavior introduces various political tactics such as building coalitions, using informational control, and leveraging trade-offs. Leaders learn through guided discussions how each tactic can be used in different organizational scenarios.
- **Impact:**
- This training helps leaders recognize and develop the necessary political skills to advance their projects and initiatives within the organization, enhancing their influence and effectiveness.

1. **Role-Playing Political Scenarios:**

- **Activity:**
- Leaders engage in role-playing exercises designed to mimic typical political situations they might face, such as securing resources, influencing key stakeholders, or navigating inter-departmental conflicts.
- **Impact:**
- By acting out these scenarios, leaders practice using political tactics in a controlled, reflective environment,

gaining confidence in their ability to handle complex political dynamics.

1. **Strategy Development Workshop:**

- **Activity:**
- In small groups, leaders work together to develop strategies for hypothetical but plausible organizational challenges. They use political mapping techniques to identify key players, potential allies, and opponents, and plan how to win support and build consensus.
- **Impact:**
- This workshop emphasizes strategic planning and foresight in using political tactics, equipping leaders with a toolkit to analyze and strategize their actions within the political landscape of the company.

1. **Ethical Boundaries Discussion:**

- **Activity:**
- A roundtable discussion facilitated by an ethics expert focuses on the ethical implications of political behavior in business. Leaders explore where to draw the line between effective politics and unethical manipulation.
- **Impact:**
- This crucial conversation helps leaders understand the importance of maintaining integrity and trust while engaging in organizational politics, ensuring that their actions contribute positively to the corporate culture and values.

At the close of the workshop, Elena brings everyone together to reflect on their learnings and discuss how these strategies can be implemented with integrity at OptiTech. She stresses the importance of continual learning and adaptation in political skills as the organizational landscape evolves.

Leaders leave the workshop with a nuanced understanding of political tactics and strategies, aware of both their power and their pitfalls. They feel better prepared to engage in organizational politics proactively and ethically.

As the leaders disperse, their thoughtful expressions and engaged postures indicate a readiness to embrace the complex, yet crucial, aspect of organizational life. Elena watches them, reassured that they are now equipped to use their enhanced political acumen to steer OptiTech through the nuanced corridors of corporate power and politics, aiming for success that is both influential and honorable.

The Ethics of Power and Politics

Building on the practical lessons from the "Mastering Organizational Politics" workshop, Elena recognizes the importance of addressing the ethical considerations surrounding power and politics in business. She organizes an "Ethics in Leadership" seminar at OptiTech's main auditorium, now set up to foster a serious and contemplative environment. The seminar is designed to engage leaders in deep discussions about the moral implications of their actions and strategies.

As the leaders of OptiTech convene in the auditorium, they find themselves in a solemn setting, conducive to reflection and thoughtful discussion. The stage is set with a panel of ethics scholars, seasoned executives, and corporate governance experts. Elena, determined to ensure that her leaders not only understand the mechanics of power but also its moral dimensions, prepares to guide them through complex ethical dilemmas that challenge even the most seasoned executives.

Elena begins the seminar by emphasizing the critical role that ethics plays in sustaining long-term organizational success. She outlines the importance of aligning power and politics with the company's core values and ethical standards, highlighting that the true measure of leadership is how power is handled when no one is watching.

Interactive Activities:

1. **Panel Discussion on Ethical Leadership:**

- **Activity:**
- A panel featuring a mix of academics and practical leaders in the field of ethics discusses the challenges and importance of ethical leadership. Topics include managing conflicts of interest, transparency, accountability, and the consequences of unethical behavior.
- **Impact:**
- This discussion provides a platform for leaders to hear different perspectives on ethical challenges, reinforcing the importance of integrity in leadership roles.

1. **Case Study Breakouts:**

- **Activity:**
- Leaders break into small groups to analyze real-world case studies involving ethical dilemmas related to power

and political maneuvers. Each group is tasked with proposing solutions that uphold ethical standards while achieving business objectives.
- **Impact:**
- Working through these scenarios helps leaders practice applying ethical frameworks to complex situations, enhancing their ability to navigate moral gray areas effectively.

1. **Ethics Training Workshop:**

- **Activity:**
- An interactive workshop led by ethics trainers who introduce various ethical decision-making models and tools that leaders can apply in their day-to-day management decisions.
- **Impact:**
- Leaders learn practical methods for incorporating ethical considerations into their decision-making processes, ensuring that their actions align with the broader values of the organization.

1. **Role-Playing Ethical Dilemmas:**

- **Activity:**
- Leaders engage in role-playing exercises designed to simulate high-pressure situations where they must balance political savvy with ethical considerations.
- **Impact:**
- These role-playing scenarios help leaders develop the skills to maintain their moral compass under pressure,

preparing them to act decisively and ethically in real situations.

At the close of the seminar, Elena gathers all participants for a final reflection. She encourages leaders to continuously engage with ethical questions and to seek guidance and feedback when faced with challenging decisions. Elena stresses that ethical leadership is a journey that requires vigilance, courage, and an unwavering commitment to doing what is right, not just what is expedient.

The leaders leave the seminar with a strengthened understanding of how to integrate ethics into their exercise of power and engagement in politics. They are reminded of the profound impact their choices have on the culture and reputation of OptiTech.

As the leaders exit the auditorium, their determined and thoughtful expressions reflect a renewed commitment to ethical leadership. Elena watches them, reassured that OptiTech's leadership is well-equipped to lead with integrity, fostering a culture of trust and respect that will drive the company towards sustainable success.

Managing Political Behavior Effectively

After deepening the understanding of ethical considerations in power and politics, Elena shifts her focus toward practical management strategies for political behavior within OptiTech. Recognizing the necessity of skillful management in this area, she sets up a strategic workshop titled "Navigating Organizational Politics." This workshop is held in OptiTech's sleek, modern conference center, designed to facilitate both open discussions and private reflection, equipped with technology for interactive presentations and real-time feedback.

The leaders of OptiTech gather in the conference center, a space transformed into a series of vignettes that represent various political landscapes within a corporate setting. Each vignette offers a different challenge, from alliance-building to navigating rivalries, and is designed to help leaders practice managing political behavior in a controlled, yet realistic environment. Elena, intent on providing her team with the tools to manage not just the work but also the workplace, prepares to guide them through understanding and applying effective political strategies.

Elena begins the workshop by outlining the often-overlooked skills needed to manage political behavior effectively. She discusses the importance of political savvy—a nuanced understanding of what motivates people and how to influence them without coercion. Elena emphasizes that this workshop is not about winning at all costs but about fostering a politically healthy environment that supports the company's goals and values.

Interactive Activities:

1. **Political Savvy Training:**

- **Activity:**
- A leadership coach introduces concepts of political savvy, including reading organizational dynamics, understanding informal networks, and the art of influence without authority. Through interactive exercises, leaders learn to map the political terrain of their environment and

identify key influencers.
- **Impact:**
- Leaders develop an enhanced awareness of the underlying currents within OptiTech, enabling them to anticipate challenges and opportunities more effectively.

1. **Scenario-Based Simulations:**

- **Activity:**
- Leaders participate in high-stakes simulations that require them to use their newly learned political skills to navigate complex scenarios. They must balance competing interests, make trade-offs, and secure buy-in for their initiatives.
- **Impact:**
- These simulations provide practical experience in managing political behavior and demonstrate the consequences of different approaches in a risk-free setting.

1. **Roundtable Discussions on Political Challenges:**

- **Activity:**
- Leaders share personal experiences and challenges related to organizational politics in a moderated discussion format. These sessions are aimed at fostering openness and collective learning.
- **Impact:**
- Sharing experiences helps leaders learn from each other's successes and mistakes, building a toolkit of strategies for managing politics at work.

1. **Action Planning for Political Management:**

- **Activity:**
- In the final part of the workshop, leaders create personalized action plans for applying political management strategies within their teams. Facilitators help leaders set specific, measurable goals for improving the political health of their departments.
- **Impact:**
- Leaders leave with a clear plan to implement strategies that manage political behavior effectively, aiming to enhance collaboration and reduce conflicts.

At the end of the workshop, Elena brings everyone together to emphasize the importance of continuous improvement and learning in the art of political management. She encourages leaders to maintain integrity and respect for individual differences while managing political behaviors, ensuring that politics never undermines the organizational culture or ethical standards.

The leaders leave the workshop equipped with both theoretical knowledge and practical skills in political management. They feel prepared to handle and harness political dynamics in ways that support OptiTech's strategic objectives and foster a healthy organizational culture.

As the leaders disperse, engaging in thoughtful discussions about their new strategies, Elena feels a sense of accomplishment. She is confident that these leaders are now better prepared to navigate the complex web of organizational politics with skill, tact, and ethical clarity, driving OptiTech toward continued success and harmony.

9

Chapter 9: Conflict and Negotiation

Buoyed by the success of the workshop on managing political behavior effectively, Elena decides to address another critical aspect of leadership and organizational dynamics: conflict and negotiation. Understanding that conflicts are inevitable in any growing company like OptiTech, she organizes a comprehensive "Conflict Resolution and Negotiation Skills" retreat at a tranquil resort located on the outskirts of the city. The retreat is equipped with seminar rooms for lectures and open spaces for role-playing exercises designed to practice negotiation techniques and conflict resolution strategies.

As OptiTech leaders arrive at the scenic resort, surrounded by peaceful woods and serene lake views, they find themselves in an environment that contrasts sharply with their daily corporate setting. This change of scenery is purposefully chosen by Elena to encourage open minds and new perspectives. The retreat is designed not only to teach effective conflict management and negotiation skills but also to allow leaders to practice these skills in real-time scenarios.

CHAPTER 9: CONFLICT AND NEGOTIATION

Elena opens the retreat with a compelling discussion on the nature of conflict in business environments, emphasizing that when managed properly, conflict can lead to growth and innovation. She outlines the structure of the retreat, which will cover different negotiation styles, conflict resolution techniques, and how to apply these in both internal and external negotiations.

Interactive Activities:

1. **Negotiation Styles Workshop:**

   - **Activity:**
   - An expert in negotiation conducts a workshop explaining different negotiation styles—from competitive to collaborative—and their appropriateness in various scenarios. Leaders assess their own default styles and participate in exercises to develop flexibility in their negotiation approaches.
   - **Impact:**
   - Leaders learn to adapt their negotiation tactics based on the situation, improving their ability to achieve favorable outcomes while maintaining strong relationships.

1. **Conflict Resolution Role-Playing:**

   - **Activity:**
   - Leaders engage in role-playing exercises that simulate typical workplace conflicts they might encounter. Scenarios include inter-departmental disputes, project management issues, and personnel conflicts. Trained facilitators

observe and provide feedback.
- **Impact:**
- These role-plays help leaders practice applying conflict resolution strategies in a controlled environment, enhancing their confidence and competence in handling real conflicts.

1. **Advanced Negotiation Simulations:**

- **Activity:**
- Leaders participate in advanced negotiation simulations involving multiple parties and complex issues, such as negotiating contracts with suppliers or forming strategic partnerships. These simulations are designed to be highly challenging to push leaders to utilize both their analytical and interpersonal skills.
- **Impact:**
- This activity sharpens leaders' negotiation skills under pressure, teaching them to think strategically and maintain poise in high-stakes situations.

1. **Debriefing and Reflection Sessions:**

- **Activity:**
- At the end of each day, leaders gather for debriefing sessions where they discuss what they learned, share insights, and reflect on how they can apply these skills in their roles at OptiTech.
- **Impact:**
- These reflections help consolidate learning and ensure leaders are prepared to translate new skills into effective

practices at work.

As the retreat concludes, Elena gathers all participants around the tranquil lakeside for a final reflection. She emphasizes the importance of continual learning and practice in the areas of conflict and negotiation, encouraging leaders to foster an environment at OptiTech where healthy conflict is seen as an opportunity for improvement and growth.

The leaders leave the retreat with a deepened understanding of conflict dynamics and enhanced negotiation skills. They feel equipped to handle disputes constructively and negotiate effectively, crucial skills for leading a dynamic and innovative tech company.

Watching her team head back to the city, refreshed and inspired, Elena feels a sense of accomplishment. She is confident that the skills her leaders have honed here will greatly enhance their ability to guide OptiTech through the complexities of business challenges, ensuring the company not only survives but thrives through inevitable conflicts and negotiations.

Types of Conflict in Organizations

After the retreat on conflict resolution and negotiation skills, Elena plans a focused seminar back at OptiTech to delve deeper into the specific types of conflict that organizations commonly face. She organizes the seminar in the main conference hall at OptiTech, transforming it into a learning center with distinct areas each designed to represent a different type of organizational conflict: interpersonal, intergroup, and structural. This setup is intended to help leaders identify, understand, and strategize responses to various conflict scenarios.

As the leaders of OptiTech enter the conference hall, they are greeted by setups that simulate real-world conflicts. Each station is equipped with interactive tools and scenario-based learning modules that depict typical workplace conflicts. Elena, committed to enhancing her team's ability to diagnose and effectively manage different types of conflict, prepares to guide them through a comprehensive exploration of conflict dynamics.

Elena opens the seminar by emphasizing the inevitability of conflict in any dynamic organization and the importance of understanding its nature to manage it effectively. She explains that the day's activities will focus on identifying the root causes of various conflicts and developing appropriate strategies for each type.

Interactive Activities:

1. **Interpersonal Conflict Workshop:**

- **Activity:**
- Leaders engage in role-playing exercises that simulate common interpersonal conflicts, such as disagreements over project management or clashes in communication styles. Facilitators provide feedback and coaching on techniques to resolve these conflicts, focusing on communication skills and emotional intelligence.
- **Impact:**
- This workshop helps leaders develop a hands-on understanding of how to handle interpersonal conflicts,

emphasizing empathy, active listening, and assertive communication.

1. **Intergroup Conflict Simulation:**

- **Activity:**
- In this simulation, leaders are divided into groups representing different departments within OptiTech. They are given a complex project that requires cross-departmental collaboration but also naturally leads to resource conflicts and priority clashes.
- **Impact:**
- Leaders experience firsthand the complexities of intergroup conflict, learning strategies to foster cooperation and align group goals.

1. **Structural Conflict Analysis:**

- **Activity:**
- Leaders analyze case studies that illustrate structural conflicts caused by organizational policies or market changes affecting the company structure. They work in teams to propose solutions that minimize conflict and adapt the organization to new realities.
- **Impact:**
- This analysis improves leaders' abilities to recognize and address structural issues that could lead to conflict, focusing on adaptive strategies and proactive organizational design.

1. **Conflict Style Assessments:**

- **Activity:**
- Each leader completes a conflict style assessment to identify their personal conflict management style. Facilitators lead discussions on how different styles impact conflict outcomes and how to adapt styles to suit various situations.
- **Impact:**
- Understanding personal conflict styles helps leaders manage their reactions in conflict situations more effectively, tailoring their approach to achieve more positive outcomes.

As the seminar concludes, Elena brings everyone together to discuss the insights gained and how these can be applied to improve OptiTech's operations and culture. She stresses that effectively managing conflict requires continuous learning and practice, urging leaders to remain committed to developing their conflict resolution skills.

The leaders leave the seminar with a clearer understanding of the specific types of conflicts that occur in organizations and the tools to manage them effectively. They are better prepared to lead their teams through challenges, turning potential conflicts into opportunities for growth and innovation.

As the participants disperse, engaged in thoughtful discussions about the day's learnings, Elena feels assured that OptiTech is becoming a stronger, more resilient organization capable of navigating the complexities of workplace conflict with skill and understanding.

The Conflict Process Model

After exploring the types of conflicts within organizations, Elena sees the need to deepen the understanding of how conflicts evolve and can be resolved over time. She schedules a workshop specifically designed to dissect and analyze the conflict process model. This workshop, held in one of OptiTech's strategic meeting rooms, is set up with stations representing each stage of the conflict process model: potential opposition or incompatibility, cognition and personalization, intentions, behavior, and outcomes.

As OptiTech leaders gather in the meeting room, they find it segmented into areas that sequentially represent the stages of the conflict process model. Each station is equipped with multimedia presentations, interactive simulations, and facilitated discussion areas. Elena, intent on providing her leaders with a clear roadmap for navigating conflict from inception to resolution, prepares to guide them through each phase with detailed explanations and hands-on activities.

Elena begins the workshop by emphasizing the importance of understanding the conflict process as a dynamic series of interactions that can escalate or de-escalate based on how they are managed. She explains that mastering this model can help leaders not only resolve conflicts more effectively but also prevent many disputes from reaching detrimental stages.

Interactive Activities:

1. **Stage 1: Potential Opposition or Incompatibility**

- **Activity:**
- Leaders identify potential sources of conflict within their teams using interactive tools that simulate workplace scenarios. They discuss these triggers in small groups, identifying early signs of opposition or incompatibility.
- **Impact:**
- This exercise helps leaders become proactive in recognizing conflict triggers early, setting the stage for timely intervention.

1. **Stage 2: Cognition and Personalization**

- **Activity:**
- Leaders reflect on how they perceive conflicts and personalize these perceptions in role-playing exercises. Facilitators help them understand the importance of separating personal feelings from professional issues.
- **Impact:**
- By exploring this stage, leaders learn to manage their emotions and perceptions, which are crucial for effective conflict resolution.

1. **Stage 3: Intentions**

- **Activity:**
- Participants engage in a workshop to explore different conflict-handling intentions, such as competing, collab-

orating, compromising, avoiding, and accommodating. They practice identifying the most appropriate intention based on different conflict scenarios.
- **Impact:**
- This activity enhances leaders' strategic decision-making in conflict situations, helping them choose the most constructive approaches.

1. **Stage 4: Behavior**

- **Activity:**
- In this segment, leaders participate in advanced role-playing scenarios that require them to act out conflicts using the intentions previously discussed. Observers give feedback on the effectiveness of behaviors in escalating or de-escalating conflicts.
- **Impact:**
- Leaders experience firsthand how their actions can influence the direction of a conflict, gaining insights into more effective conflict management behaviors.

1. **Stage 5: Outcomes**

- **Activity:**
- Leaders analyze the outcomes of role-play scenarios to determine whether the conflict led to a functional or dysfunctional resolution. They discuss how different resolutions can impact team performance and morale.
- **Impact:**
- Understanding the outcomes helps leaders appreciate the long-term effects of conflict management and strives

to achieve resolutions that benefit team cohesion and productivity.

At the close of the workshop, Elena brings everyone together to reflect on the lessons learned and discuss how they can apply the conflict process model in their day-to-day management practices. She emphasizes the value of a systematic approach to conflict, encouraging her leaders to implement these strategies to foster a more collaborative and supportive work environment.

The leaders leave the workshop with a comprehensive understanding of the conflict process model and practical experience in managing each stage effectively. They are better equipped to handle workplace conflicts constructively, promoting a healthier organizational culture.

As the leaders leave the workshop, engaged and thoughtful, Elena feels confident that they are now better prepared to manage conflicts with skill and insight. This training not only equips them to handle current challenges but also empowers them to lead OptiTech toward a future marked by collaborative success and fewer disruptive conflicts.

Strategies for Conflict Resolution

Following the detailed exploration of the conflict process model, Elena decides to focus on equipping her leaders with specific, actionable strategies for resolving conflicts effectively. To facilitate this, she organizes a "Conflict Resolution Strategies Workshop" in OptiTech's newly designed collaborative space, equipped with mediation rooms, negotiation simulations, and technology for virtual reality conflict scenarios.

As the leaders gather in the collaborative space, they find themselves in an environment tailored to foster understanding, communication, and resolution. Each corner of the room is set up to practice different resolution strategies such as mediation, negotiation, arbitration, and conciliation. Elena, committed to transforming how conflicts are handled at OptiTech, prepares to guide the leaders through a series of activities designed to build their skills and confidence in conflict resolution.

Elena begins the workshop by emphasizing the importance of viewing conflict as an opportunity for growth and improvement. She outlines the various strategies that will be explored during the workshop, each tailored to different types of conflicts and situations. Her goal is to ensure that every leader leaves with a toolkit of conflict resolution strategies that they can adapt to their needs.

Interactive Activities:

1. **Mediation Role-Playing:**

- **Activity:**
- Leaders participate in role-playing exercises where they act as both mediators and disputants, working through scripted scenarios that reflect common conflicts within OptiTech. They practice facilitating discussions, guiding parties toward mutual understanding and compromise.
- **Impact:**
- This activity helps leaders learn the art of mediation, emphasizing active listening, empathy, and creating win-

win solutions.

1. **Negotiation Simulations:**

- **Activity:**
- Using negotiation tables equipped with real-time feedback mechanisms, leaders engage in negotiation exercises. They are tasked with achieving specific objectives while also maintaining or improving relationship metrics displayed on their feedback devices.
- **Impact:**
- Leaders hone their negotiation skills, learning how to balance assertiveness with cooperativeness, and understanding the importance of preparation and adaptability in negotiations.

1. **Arbitration Panels:**

- **Activity:**
- Leaders observe and participate in mock arbitration sessions where a neutral arbitrator hears both sides of a conflict and makes a decision. This scenario is used for more serious conflicts where mediation and negotiation have not been successful.
- **Impact:**
- This session introduces leaders to the arbitration process, highlighting when and how it should be used as a conflict resolution strategy.

1. **Conciliation Workshops:**

- **Activity:**
- In conciliation workshops, leaders practice the role of a conciliator who facilitates dialogue and negotiation but also suggests solutions for disputing parties to consider, differing from mediation by being more directive.
- **Impact:**
- Leaders learn another method of conflict resolution that can be effective when parties need more guidance to reach a resolution.

As the workshop concludes, Elena gathers all the participants to discuss their experiences and insights from the day. She stresses the importance of choosing the right strategy based on the specific context and dynamics of the conflict and encourages ongoing practice and learning in these areas.

The leaders leave the workshop equipped with a comprehensive understanding of various conflict resolution strategies and the confidence to implement them effectively within their teams.

As the leaders disperse, their engaged discussions and thoughtful expressions show Elena that they are now better prepared to handle conflicts constructively. She feels confident that these enhanced skills will lead to a more harmonious and productive workplace at OptiTech, where conflicts are managed effectively and turned into opportunities for improvement.

Role of Negotiation in Conflict Resolution

With the OptiTech leaders now familiar with various conflict resolution strategies, Elena decides to zero in on the crucial role of negotiation, often the linchpin in resolving conflicts effectively. To explore this further, she organizes a "Negotiation Mastery Seminar" in OptiTech's main auditorium, converted into a high-tech negotiation training facility complete with digital negotiation tables, real-time feedback displays, and stations for observing and analyzing negotiation tactics.

As OptiTech's leaders enter the auditorium, they are met with an environment that simulates intense negotiation settings, designed to mirror the complexities and pressures of real-world business negotiations. Elena, determined to deepen her team's negotiation skills, has planned a comprehensive program that integrates advanced negotiation theories with practical exercises, ensuring that every leader can master these essential skills.

Elena begins the seminar by discussing the significance of negotiation as a primary tool in conflict resolution. She emphasizes that negotiation skills are critical not just for resolving disputes but also for everyday interactions and decisions that require consensus and cooperation. She outlines the seminar's objectives, focusing on understanding interests versus positions, mastering negotiation techniques, and developing strategies to achieve optimal outcomes.

Interactive Activities:

1. **Negotiation Fundamentals Workshop:**

- **Activity:**
- An expert in negotiation theory presents the foundational concepts of effective negotiation, including the difference between positional bargaining and interest-based negotiation. Leaders learn to identify underlying interests in a conflict rather than focusing solely on surface positions.
- **Impact:**
- This workshop helps leaders understand the importance of uncovering and addressing real interests to find more durable and satisfying resolutions to conflicts.

1. **High-Stakes Negotiation Simulations:**

- **Activity:**
- Leaders participate in simulated negotiations that involve complex scenarios typical of OptiTech's business environment. These simulations include multi-party deals, tight deadlines, and significant resource implications.
- **Impact:**
- Participants apply negotiation techniques in a controlled, high-pressure environment, learning to maintain composure, use persuasive communication, and apply strategic concessions.

1. **Real-Time Analysis and Feedback:**

- **Activity:**

- During the simulations, negotiations are recorded and analyzed in real-time by negotiation experts who provide immediate feedback and coaching. This feedback focuses on body language, tone, choice of words, and strategy effectiveness.
- **Impact:**
- Leaders receive personalized insights into their negotiation style and practical advice on how to improve their tactics, enhancing their ability to influence outcomes positively.

1. **Strategy Development Lab:**

- **Activity:**
- Leaders use the insights and skills gained from earlier sessions to develop their negotiation strategies for upcoming real-world conflicts and opportunities at OptiTech. They work in teams to create comprehensive plans and role-play scenarios to test their strategies.
- **Impact:**
- This lab allows leaders to think critically about how they can implement their negotiation skills to support both their personal leadership goals and the broader objectives of OptiTech.

As the seminar concludes, Elena brings everyone together to reflect on the day's learnings. She emphasizes the transformative power of skilled negotiation in resolving conflicts and advancing organizational goals. Elena encourages leaders to continue practicing and refining their negotiation skills, considering them essential tools for their leadership toolkit.

The leaders leave the seminar with enhanced negotiation abilities, equipped with both the theoretical knowledge and practical skills necessary to navigate and resolve conflicts effectively. They appreciate the critical role negotiation plays in creating value for all parties involved.

As the leaders depart, energized by their new skills and the potential impacts on their professional roles, Elena feels confident that they are better prepared to handle the complexities of negotiation and conflict resolution. She trusts that these enhanced skills will lead to more collaborative and productive outcomes across OptiTech, fostering a culture of understanding and mutual respect.

Best Practices for Successful Negotiation

Encouraged by the progress made in the "Negotiation Mastery Seminar," Elena decides to further refine her leaders' negotiation skills by hosting a specialized workshop called "Best Practices for Successful Negotiation." This session is designed to consolidate their learning and focus on the application of industry-leading negotiation tactics. The workshop is set up in OptiTech's executive training room, now resembling a corporate boardroom environment conducive to serious negotiation training, with stations for role-playing, peer reviews, and expert panels.

As the OptiTech leaders enter the executive training room, they find a professional setup waiting for them, complete with negotiation tables, multimedia presentations, and areas designated for small group discussions. Elena, aiming to arm her leaders with the most effective and up-to-date negotiation practices, has organized a day filled with activities that emphasize practical application and continuous improvement.

Elena starts the workshop by highlighting the significance of adopting best practices in negotiation, not just to achieve immediate goals but to build and maintain long-term business relationships. She stresses the importance of preparation, strategy, and adaptability in becoming a successful negotiator.

Interactive Activities:

1. **Masterclass on Preparation Techniques:**

   - **Activity:**
   - A negotiation expert leads a masterclass on the crucial role of preparation, teaching techniques for gathering information, understanding the opponent's needs, and setting clear, achievable objectives.
   - **Impact:**
   - Leaders learn to approach negotiations with a comprehensive preparation strategy, ensuring they enter any negotiation scenario with a solid foundation and clear goals.

1. **Interactive Role-Playing Scenarios:**

   - **Activity:**
   - Leaders engage in advanced role-playing exercises that simulate challenging negotiation scenarios across various contexts. These scenarios require them to apply the best practices discussed, with observers providing real-time feedback.
   - **Impact:**

- This hands-on experience allows leaders to practice and refine their negotiation techniques in a dynamic, responsive environment, enhancing their adaptability and strategy execution skills.

1. **Panel Discussion on Ethical Negotiation:**

- **Activity:**
- A panel of ethics experts discusses the importance of maintaining integrity and fairness in negotiations. The discussion covers how to handle ethical dilemmas and the long-term benefits of ethical negotiation practices.
- **Impact:**
- Leaders are reminded of the importance of ethics in negotiation, reinforcing the company's commitment to integrity and building trust with partners and stakeholders.

1. **Feedback and Continuous Improvement Session:**

- **Activity:**
- Leaders receive personalized feedback based on their performance in role-playing scenarios. They also learn how to give constructive feedback and use it to foster continuous improvement in their negotiation skills.
- **Impact:**
- This session encourages a culture of feedback and continuous learning within OptiTech, with leaders learning not only to improve their own skills but also to help their peers improve.

At the close of the workshop, Elena gathers everyone for a final debrief, encouraging them to integrate the day's learnings into their everyday negotiation practices. She emphasizes that negotiation is not just about winning a deal but also about forging relationships that bring value to all parties involved over time.

The leaders leave the workshop equipped with a toolkit of best practices for successful negotiation, feeling more confident and prepared to handle complex negotiations that drive OptiTech forward.

As the leaders depart, their lively discussions and enthusiastic plans for applying what they've learned show Elena that OptiTech is on a strong path toward fostering a cadre of skilled, ethical negotiators. She is confident that these enhanced negotiation skills will lead to better outcomes for the company, fostering growth and stability in the competitive tech industry.

Case Studies on Conflict and Negotiation

To deepen the understanding of conflict resolution and negotiation techniques, Elena decides to leverage real-world experiences by introducing a series of case studies. She organizes a "Case Studies Day" at OptiTech, transforming the main auditorium into a dynamic classroom setting. Each section of the room is dedicated to discussing a different high-profile corporate case study, complete with detailed analyses, multimedia presentations, and breakout groups for in-depth discussion.

As the OptiTech leaders gather in the auditorium, they find themselves surrounded by setups for various famous negotiation scenarios ranging from mergers and acquisitions to labor disputes and international trade agreements. Elena, knowing the power of practical examples to illustrate complex concepts, has selected cases that highlight both successful and problematic approaches to conflict and negotiation.

Elena begins the day by emphasizing the value of learning from real-life situations. She explains that the chosen case studies will serve as practical examples of how negotiation strategies and conflict resolution techniques can be applied under different circumstances, and what can be learned from each outcome.

Interactive Activities:

1. **Apple vs. Samsung Patent Dispute:**

- **Activity:**
- Leaders examine the multi-national legal battles between Apple and Samsung over intellectual property. This case study focuses on the negotiation tactics used by each side, the escalation of conflict, and the eventual settlements.
- **Impact:**
- This discussion highlights the complexities of negotiation in a highly competitive tech industry, underscoring the importance of strategic preparation and the potential costs of prolonged conflict.

1. **Disney's Acquisition of Pixar:**

- **Activity:**
- This case study explores the negotiations that led to

Disney's acquisition of Pixar, emphasizing the role of building relationships and aligning organizational cultures in successful negotiations.
- **Impact:**
- Leaders learn how integrating interests and fostering mutual respect can lead to agreements that benefit all parties and support long-term collaboration.

1. **The Cuban Missile Crisis:**

- **Activity:**
- Considered one of the highest stakes negotiations in history, this case study allows leaders to analyze the negotiation strategies used by the United States and the Soviet Union to de-escalate a potentially catastrophic conflict.
- **Impact:**
- This case study teaches the critical importance of diplomacy, back-channel communications, and the careful balancing of threats and concessions in conflict resolution.

1. **The Writers Guild of America Strike:**

- **Activity:**
- Leaders delve into the 2007–2008 strike by the Writers Guild of America, focusing on the negotiations between writers and major American television studios. The discussion centers on collective bargaining, the power of unions, and strategic negotiation in labor disputes.
- **Impact:**
- The case offers insights into managing group conflicts,

the dynamics of power in negotiations, and the impact of public opinion and solidarity in achieving favorable outcomes.

As the day concludes, Elena brings everyone together to reflect on what they've learned from these diverse scenarios. She encourages leaders to think critically about the negotiation strategies and conflict resolution techniques that could be applied within OptiTech.

The leaders leave the event with a deeper understanding of how to approach complex negotiations and resolve conflicts effectively. They appreciate the real-world applications of the strategies discussed and feel better prepared to apply these lessons to their daily challenges.

Watching her team engage in animated discussions as they exit the auditorium, Elena is satisfied that the case studies have provided them with valuable lessons on negotiation and conflict resolution. She feels confident that these insights will empower her leaders to manage future conflicts more effectively and negotiate deals that align with OptiTech's strategic goals and ethical standards.

10

Chapter 10: Organizational Culture

With the workshops on conflict and negotiation adding robust tools to her team's arsenal, Elena turns her focus toward strengthening OptiTech's foundational elements—its organizational culture. To deepen the understanding and appreciation of OptiTech's culture, Elena organizes a two-day retreat titled "Cultivating Our Culture," set in a picturesque mountain lodge that provides a natural and serene backdrop conducive to introspection and community building.

As OptiTech's leaders arrive at the lodge, surrounded by lush greenery and breathtaking mountain views, they find a retreat setting designed to foster open communication, collaboration, and reflection. The retreat includes interactive workshops, group discussions, and cultural immersion activities intended to embody and reinforce the core values and behaviors that make up OptiTech's unique organizational culture.

Elena begins the retreat with a heartfelt speech about the importance of organizational culture in driving innovation,

lieve should define OptiTech. This includes defining what each value means in daily operations and interactions.
- **Impact:**
- This workshop helps distill the core values that resonate most with employees, ensuring that the defined culture aligns with both employee beliefs and business objectives.

1. **Storytelling Roundtables:**

- **Activity:**
- Employees share personal stories that highlight moments when OptiTech's culture was particularly evident. These stories help illustrate the impact of culture on individual and team experiences.
- **Impact:**
- Storytelling not only fosters a deeper emotional connection to the culture but also illustrates real-life examples of the culture in action, reinforcing the values and behaviors that make OptiTech unique.

1. **Future Culture Vision Boards:**

- **Activity:**
- Participants create vision boards that represent their hopes and visions for the future of OptiTech's culture. These boards incorporate ideas on how the culture can evolve to support changing market dynamics and employee needs.
- **Impact:**
- This creative activity allows employees to express their aspirations for the culture, contributing to a forward-

looking approach that embraces growth and change.

As the seminar concludes, Elena brings everyone together for a collective reflection session. She emphasizes the importance of everyone's contribution to defining and shaping the culture, encouraging continuous dialogue and involvement from all employees.

Employees leave the seminar with a clear understanding of what defines OptiTech's culture, feeling empowered and responsible for nurturing and protecting the values and behaviors that they have collectively endorsed.

Watching her team engage in animated discussions and proudly display their vision boards, Elena feels a profound sense of accomplishment. She knows that this collective effort to define and understand their culture is the first step toward ensuring that OptiTech remains a vibrant, cohesive, and resilient organization well into the future.

Models of Organizational Culture

Following the successful "Defining Our Culture" seminars, Elena decides to deepen the understanding of organizational culture at OptiTech by exploring various theoretical models that explain how cultures develop and function within companies. She organizes a series of educational workshops titled "Exploring Models of Organizational Culture" in the main conference hall, now arranged to facilitate learning with multimedia presentations and discussion zones.

As OptiTech leaders and selected employees from various departments gather in the conference hall, they find it equipped with resources for a deep dive into some of the most influential models of organizational culture. Elena, aiming to equip her team with a more structured understanding of cultural frameworks, prepares to guide them through theories that will help them analyze and enhance their own organizational culture effectively.

Elena starts the workshop by stressing the importance of understanding different models of organizational culture as a way to gain insights into their own practices and behaviors. She explains that these models can serve as lenses through which to view their current culture, identify what drives it, and determine how it can be directed towards strategic goals.

Interactive Activities:

1. **Edgar Schein's Model Exploration:**

- **Activity:**
- A deep dive into Edgar Schein's Three Levels of Culture: Artifacts, Espoused Values, and Basic Underlying Assumptions. Leaders and employees analyze each level in the context of OptiTech, using interactive polls and discussions to map out visible artifacts, stated values, and underlying assumptions.
- **Impact:**
- This framework helps participants understand the depth of cultural elements and how they manifest in everyday operations, influencing behavior and decision-making at OptiTech.

1. **Hofstede's Cultural Dimensions Theory:**

- **Activity:**
- Exploration of Geert Hofstede's Dimensions of Culture, which includes Individualism vs. Collectivism, Uncertainty Avoidance, Power Distance, Masculinity vs. Femininity, Long-Term Orientation, and Indulgence vs. Restraint. Participants assess where OptiTech stands on each dimension through group discussions and scenario analysis.
- **Impact:**
- Understanding these dimensions aids in recognizing the broader cultural dynamics that influence organizational interactions both internally and with international partners.

1. **Denison's Organizational Culture Model:**

- **Activity:**
- Examination of Daniel Denison's model which focuses on four cultural traits: Mission, Consistency, Involvement, and Adaptability. Leaders work in groups to evaluate how well OptiTech embodies each trait and devise plans to strengthen areas that are lacking.
- **Impact:**
- This model provides a clear structure for aligning organizational culture with business strategy, emphasizing the practical implications of culture on performance and adaptability.

1. **The Competing Values Framework:**

- **Activity:**

- Interactive sessions on the Competing Values Framework that categorizes organizational culture into four types: Clan, Adhocracy, Market, and Hierarchy. Employees identify the dominant culture at OptiTech and discuss the benefits and challenges of each type.
- **Impact:**
- Participants learn how different cultural types affect management style, employee engagement, and the company's ability to innovate and compete in the market.

At the end of the workshop, Elena facilitates a group reflection on the insights gained and how these models can guide their efforts to cultivate a supportive and dynamic organizational culture. She encourages continued education and application of these cultural frameworks to enhance strategic alignment and organizational health.

The participants leave the workshop with a sophisticated toolkit of cultural models, each offering different perspectives on how to understand and shape the organizational environment at OptiTech. They appreciate the complexity and power of culture in driving organizational success.

As the teams disperse, their animated conversations signal a renewed commitment to leveraging these cultural insights. Elena watches, satisfied with the knowledge that these frameworks will provide a solid foundation for ongoing cultural development at OptiTech, ensuring it remains a vibrant and progressive workplace.

The Role of Leaders in Cultivating Culture

With a solid understanding of various models of organizational culture now embedded within OptiTech's leadership, Elena feels it's crucial to emphasize the pivotal role leaders play in cultivating and sustaining these cultural dynamics. To this end, she organizes a special leadership summit called "Leaders as Culture Champions" at a contemporary conference center downtown, which has been set up to encourage open dialogue and collaborative planning.

As OptiTech's leaders convene in the bright, modern conference center, they find themselves surrounded by banners and visuals emphasizing key cultural values such as innovation, integrity, teamwork, and customer focus. Elena, determined to solidify the leadership's role as the primary drivers and custodians of OptiTech's culture, has prepared a program that combines expert talks, peer discussions, and strategic workshops focused on culture leadership.

Elena begins the summit by articulating the critical influence leaders have on organizational culture, whether through direct actions or the norms and expectations they set. She outlines how today's sessions will help them develop actionable strategies to not only embody but also propagate these cultural values throughout the organization.

Interactive Activities:

1. **Leadership and Culture Alignment Workshops:**

- **Activity:**
- Leaders engage in workshops to align their personal lead-

ership styles with OptiTech's desired cultural attributes. Facilitators help them identify any gaps and explore strategies to modify their leadership approaches to better reflect and reinforce organizational values.
- **Impact:**
- This activity ensures that leaders are not just aware of, but fully aligned with, the cultural goals of OptiTech, ready to lead by example and inspire the same commitment in their teams.

1. **Storytelling for Cultural Advocacy:**

- **Activity:**
- A session on the power of storytelling where leaders learn to craft and share stories that highlight core cultural values in action. These stories are geared to be used in team meetings, company communications, and external engagements.
- **Impact:**
- Leaders harness the emotional and mnemonic power of storytelling to reinforce culture, making the abstract notions of cultural values tangible and memorable for all employees.

1. **Cultural Champions Initiative Launch:**

- **Activity:**
- Elena introduces a new initiative where leaders identify and mentor 'Cultural Champions' from within their teams who exemplify and can further disseminate OptiTech's values. This program includes training and

resources for these champions.
- **Impact:**
- By empowering passionate individuals, the initiative aims to create a network of influence that supports the culture from the ground up, ensuring its sustainability and resilience.

1. **Culture Feedback and Continuous Improvement Panels:**

- **Activity:**
- Leaders participate in panel discussions that review current cultural feedback mechanisms and explore innovative ways to gather insights on the cultural health of the organization. They develop continuous improvement plans based on this feedback.
- **Impact:**
- This ensures that leadership remains responsive and adaptive, continually evolving the culture in alignment with both internal feedback and external market changes.

As the summit wraps up, Elena gathers the leaders for a closing session, where she emphasizes the ongoing nature of cultural development and the crucial role of leadership in that process. She challenges each leader to take personal responsibility for the culture they create and influence every day.

Leaders leave the summit invigorated, with clear plans and strategies to further cultivate a vibrant organizational culture. They recognize their role as both custodians and advocates of the culture, equipped with the tools to inspire and lead cultural transformation at every level of OptiTech.

As the conference center empties, the buzz of inspired conversations fills the air. Elena watches with pride and optimism, confident that her leaders are now better equipped than ever to actively shape and steer OptiTech's culture, ensuring it remains a cornerstone of their competitive advantage and organizational identity.

Culture's Impact on Performance and Satisfaction

Following the leadership summit on "Leaders as Culture Champions," Elena identifies a critical link that needs further exploration: the direct impact of organizational culture on employee performance and job satisfaction. To underscore this connection, she organizes a seminar titled "Culture Drives Performance" at OptiTech's main auditorium, now transformed into an interactive learning environment with data visualization screens, employee testimonials, and live survey results.

As OptiTech's leaders and key employees gather in the auditorium, they are greeted by an array of data dashboards showing real-time feedback and metrics from various departments. The setup is designed to visually demonstrate how deeply culture influences key performance indicators and employee morale. Elena, intent on solidifying the understanding that culture is not just a HR concern but a strategic business driver, has prepared a detailed agenda that mixes expert analysis, real OptiTech case studies, and employee-led discussions.

Elena opens the seminar with an overview of studies and organizational data that highlight the correlation between strong, positive corporate cultures and enhanced business performance and employee satisfaction. She sets the stage for a day dedicated to unpacking how OptiTech's culture directly affects its success and the well-being of its employees.

Interactive Activities:

1. **Case Study Breakdowns:**

- **Activity:**
- Leaders are presented with case studies from within OptiTech and other organizations that have successfully leveraged culture to drive performance improvements and increase employee satisfaction. Groups discuss the strategies employed and the outcomes achieved.
- **Impact:**
- These case studies provide concrete examples of how cultural initiatives can lead to measurable improvements in productivity, innovation, and employee retention.

1. **Cultural Metrics Analysis Workshop:**

- **Activity:**
- A workshop facilitated by a data analyst dives into OptiTech's own cultural metrics, linking them to performance outcomes across various teams. Leaders learn how to interpret cultural data and use it to make informed decisions.
- **Impact:**
- This hands-on analysis helps leaders understand the quantitative aspect of culture's impact, empowering them

guiding decision-making, and shaping the company's identity and public image. She shares her vision for a culture that not only drives success but also fosters a supportive and inclusive environment for all employees.

Interactive Activities:

1. **Cultural Values Workshop:**

- **Activity:**
- Leaders participate in a workshop where they examine OptiTech's current cultural values, discuss how these values are perceived and enacted in daily operations, and explore any gaps between ideal and actual behaviors.
- **Impact:**
- This session helps leaders identify strengths and areas for improvement within the current culture, providing a platform for developing actionable strategies to enhance alignment with organizational values.

1. **Cultural Artifacts Exploration:**

- **Activity:**
- In this activity, leaders explore various "artifacts" of OptiTech's culture, including internal communications, mission statements, office design, and social media presence. They analyze how these artifacts reflect the company's values and contribute to the culture.
- **Impact:**
- Leaders gain insights into how tangible and intangible elements can be leveraged to reinforce the cultural identity

and core values of OptiTech.

1. **Cultural Champions Panel:**

- **Activity:**
- A panel of employees who are considered cultural champions at OptiTech share their experiences and perspectives on what makes the culture unique and how they contribute to sustaining it.
- **Impact:**
- This discussion provides inspiration and practical examples of how every employee can be a custodian of the company culture, motivating leaders to foster and recognize cultural advocacy in their teams.

1. **Building a Culture Plan:**

- **Activity:**
- Leaders collaborate to create a culture plan that includes specific initiatives, programs, and policies aimed at strengthening areas of the culture that are aligned with OptiTech's strategic goals.
- **Impact:**
- By the end of this activity, leaders have a clear, actionable plan to enhance organizational culture, ensuring it supports both employee well-being and business objectives.

As the retreat wraps up, Elena gathers everyone for a closing circle by a large campfire outside the lodge. She encourages each leader to share their commitments to the culture plan and discusses how these commitments can be integrated into their leadership practices.

The leaders leave the retreat with a renewed commitment to nurturing and protecting OptiTech's culture. They have a deeper understanding of the role culture plays in every aspect of organizational life and are equipped with strategies to strengthen it.

As the leaders depart, their lively discussions and thoughtful reflections on the retreat's activities resonate with Elena. She feels confident that the strengthened cultural understanding and commitment will permeate through the leaders to every member of OptiTech, guiding the company to future successes built on a solid foundation of shared values and practices.

Defining Organizational Culture

After the transformative retreat focused on cultivating and enhancing OptiTech's organizational culture, Elena decides it is crucial to consolidate this learning by defining what organizational culture truly means for everyone at OptiTech. To achieve this, she organizes a series of seminars titled "Defining Our Culture," to be held at OptiTech's headquarters. Each session is designed to involve employees from different levels of the organization, ensuring that the culture is understood, shaped, and embraced by all.

As OptiTech employees gather in the main conference room, transformed into a collaborative workshop space with interactive digital boards and small group breakout areas, they are met with an atmosphere of inclusivity and openness. Elena, determined to engage every employee in the conversation about what their culture is and should be, has planned a day filled with activities that explore the depths and breadths of organizational culture.

Elena starts the seminar with an engaging talk on the importance of organizational culture as the soul of the company, driving not just business success but also employee satisfaction and engagement. She explains that the day's goal is to collectively define what makes up OptiTech's culture, identifying the key components that each employee resonates with.

Interactive Activities:

1. **Culture Mapping Session:**

- **Activity:**
- Employees participate in a guided culture mapping exercise where they identify elements that currently define OptiTech's culture. This includes beliefs, behaviors, rituals, and symbols that are prevalent within the organization.
- **Impact:**
- This session allows employees to visualize the many layers and elements of the culture, creating a shared understanding of what exists and what needs to be strengthened or changed.

1. **Values Identification Workshop:**

- **Activity:**
- Through interactive polling and group discussions, participants list and prioritize the core values that they be-

to foster data-driven cultural enhancements.

1. **Panel Discussion: Employee Perspectives:**

- **Activity:**
- A diverse panel of OptiTech employees shares personal stories about how the company culture has impacted their job satisfaction and performance. The session includes Q&A, allowing leaders to hear directly from their teams.
- **Impact:**
- This discussion bridges the gap between management perceptions and employee reality, providing insights into how culture directly affects day-to-day experiences and job enthusiasm.

1. **Strategic Culture-Enhancement Roundtables:**

- **Activity:**
- Leaders participate in roundtable discussions to devise specific strategies for enhancing areas of culture that are most strongly correlated with high performance and satisfaction. Each table tackles different aspects such as work-life balance, recognition, innovation, or collaboration.
- **Impact:**
- By focusing on targeted cultural improvements, leaders can strategically address gaps that may be hindering performance or reducing job satisfaction.

As the seminar concludes, Elena brings everyone together to reflect on the day's insights. She emphasizes the importance of continuously nurturing a culture that not only aligns with business goals but also fulfills and motivates employees. She encourages leaders to think of culture as a dynamic and powerful tool for achieving both employee satisfaction and superior business performance.

Leaders leave the seminar with a profound understanding of the tangible impact that organizational culture has on performance and satisfaction. They recognize the importance of their role in shaping a culture that not only drives success but also fosters a fulfilling work environment.

As the auditorium slowly empties, the leaders' animated discussions and committed expressions reflect their renewed dedication to cultivating a powerful organizational culture. Elena feels confident that these insights will inspire actionable changes, ensuring that OptiTech's culture continues to be a cornerstone of its success and a model for others in the industry.

Assessing and Changing Organizational Culture

After demonstrating the profound impact of organizational culture on performance and satisfaction, Elena recognizes the necessity for periodic assessment and adaptation of the culture at OptiTech. To address this, she schedules a strategic workshop titled "Evolving Our Culture," hosted in OptiTech's innovation center, now equipped with collaborative tech tools for real-time feedback, culture analytics software, and virtual reality setups for immersive cultural experiences.

As OptiTech's leaders and key cultural influencers gather in the innovation center, they find themselves in a space that embodies the cutting edge of corporate cultural assessment.

The room is segmented into various stations, each dedicated to different aspects of cultural evaluation and innovation strategies. Elena, determined to guide her team through the complexities of cultural evolution, has prepared an interactive program designed to identify areas of strength and potential growth within OptiTech's culture.

Elena opens the workshop with an engaging presentation on the dynamic nature of organizational culture. She emphasizes that as the external market environment and internal employee demographics change, so too must the culture to remain relevant and effective. She outlines the tools and strategies that will be explored during the workshop, aimed at both assessing the current cultural landscape and implementing sustainable changes.

Interactive Activities:

1. **Cultural Audit Stations:**

   - **Activity:**
   - Leaders rotate through stations equipped with surveys, interviews, and observational tools to conduct a live cultural audit. They collect data on various aspects of OptiTech's culture, including core values adherence, communication patterns, and employee engagement levels.
   - **Impact:**
   - This hands-on audit provides a snapshot of the current cultural state, identifying both high-performing areas and those requiring intervention.

1. **VR Culture Walkthroughs:**

- **Activity:**
- Participants use virtual reality to experience immersive scenarios that depict OptiTech's culture in action. These scenarios include handling conflicts, celebrating milestones, and everyday interactions among staff.
- **Impact:**
- VR walkthroughs help participants viscerally understand the employee experience, offering a unique perspective on how cultural norms and values are actually manifested in the workplace.

1. **Change Management Workshops:**

- **Activity:**
- Facilitators lead interactive sessions on change management theories and practices, particularly as they relate to shifting organizational culture. Leaders learn about models such as Lewin's Change Management Model and Kotter's 8-Step Change Model, applying them to hypothetical cultural change scenarios at OptiTech.
- **Impact:**
- Leaders gain practical knowledge on how to effectively plan, initiate, and sustain cultural changes within an organization.

1. **Action Planning Roundtables:**

- **Activity:**
- In these collaborative sessions, leaders synthesize their

findings from the day and develop strategic action plans for cultural enhancement. These plans address specific areas needing improvement, with clear goals, designated responsibilities, and timelines.
- **Impact:**
- The action plans created provide a clear roadmap for initiating and tracking cultural changes, ensuring accountability and ongoing evaluation.

As the workshop concludes, Elena gathers all participants to discuss the collective vision for OptiTech's cultural future. She emphasizes the importance of everyone's role in nurturing and evolving the culture, inspiring a shared commitment to continuous improvement.

Leaders leave the workshop equipped with a comprehensive understanding of how to assess and adapt OptiTech's culture effectively. They are empowered with tools and strategies to make informed decisions that align with both employee welfare and business objectives.

Watching her team engage passionately in their new projects, Elena feels confident that OptiTech is well on its way to fostering a culture that is not only robust and adaptive but also deeply integrated with its core mission and vision. This proactive approach to cultural evolution promises to keep OptiTech at the forefront of the industry, resilient and responsive to both internal and external changes.

Global Influences on Organizational Culture

With a strong foundation in assessing and evolving the organizational culture at OptiTech, Elena decides to address the next critical dimension—global influences. In today's interconnected world, understanding the impact of diverse cultural backgrounds on organizational culture is vital. Elena organizes a global culture summit, "Cultures Converge," at OptiTech's largest conference hall, now transformed into a global village with areas designated to represent various cultural zones from around the world.

As OptiTech's leaders and employees from international branches gather, they are greeted by a vibrant display of global cultures, each area showcasing traditional artifacts, multimedia presentations on local business practices, and interactive cultural workshops. Elena, recognizing the importance of inclusivity and diversity as key drivers of innovation and growth, has planned a comprehensive agenda to explore and integrate global perspectives into OptiTech's evolving organizational culture.

Elena starts the summit with an engaging talk on the value of global diversity and its impact on organizational culture. She explains that embracing a global perspective will not only enhance OptiTech's competitiveness but also enrich its cultural tapestry, fostering a more inclusive and dynamic workplace.

Interactive Activities:

1. **Cultural Immersion Booths:**

- **Activity:**
- Participants visit booths that simulate business environments from different parts of the world, including Asia, Europe, Africa, and the Americas. Each booth offers hands-on experiences with local business etiquettes, communication styles, and management practices.
- **Impact:**
- This immersive experience helps participants appreciate the nuances of global business cultures and understand how these differences can influence workplace dynamics and employee interactions.

1. **Panel Discussion on Global Business Challenges:**

- **Activity:**
- A diverse panel of international business leaders shares insights into overcoming cross-cultural challenges. Topics include managing multicultural teams, adapting corporate policies to local contexts, and leveraging cultural diversity for market expansion.
- **Impact:**
- Hearing directly from experienced leaders provides practical strategies for navigating global business landscapes and integrating diverse cultural insights into corporate practices.

1. **Workshop on Integrating Global Cultures:**

- **Activity:**
- Facilitators lead a workshop where participants develop integration strategies that align global cultural norms with OptiTech's core values. They work on creating inclusive policies and practices that accommodate and celebrate cultural diversity.
- **Impact:**
- This workshop enables leaders to craft actionable plans that enhance cultural cohesion and ensure that all employees, regardless of their background, feel valued and understood.

1. **Global Culture Innovation Labs:**

- **Activity:**
- In these labs, participants brainstorm new product ideas or business solutions that leverage OptiTech's diverse cultural insights. They use design thinking principles to ensure that these innovations are globally relevant and culturally sensitive.
- **Impact:**
- The innovation labs foster creativity and encourage the practical application of global cultural knowledge, driving OptiTech's growth in international markets.

As the summit concludes, Elena brings everyone together to reflect on the enriching experiences of the day. She emphasizes the competitive advantage that a globally aware and culturally diverse workforce offers and commits to making cultural inclusivity a cornerstone of OptiTech's strategic development.

Participants leave the summit with a deeper understanding of global cultural dynamics and renewed enthusiasm for embracing diversity. They are equipped with the knowledge and tools to further enrich OptiTech's culture, making it a truly global and inclusive entity.

As the conference hall slowly empties, the buzz of inspired conversations and the exchange of contact information among international colleagues signal the success of the summit. Elena watches with pride, confident that these global insights will guide OptiTech toward a future marked by cultural richness, innovation, and global market leadership.

11

Chapter 11: Change Management

With OptiTech's organizational culture well understood and a global perspective integrated, Elena recognizes the need to shift focus to navigating through the ever-changing technological landscape. OptiTech, poised to launch its groundbreaking AI product, faces internal resistance and operational challenges that threaten its strategic goals. Elena plans a comprehensive "Navigating Change" seminar at OptiTech's main campus, aimed at equipping leaders with tools and strategies for effective change management.

The seminar takes place in a large, open space transformed to simulate different business environments that may emerge as a result of the upcoming changes. Elena, aware that the successful launch and integration of the new AI technology hinge on the company's ability to manage change effectively, has curated a series of workshops, keynote speeches, and simulation exercises that mirror potential future scenarios.

Elena opens the seminar with a compelling speech about the inevitability and necessity of change, especially in the technology sector. She emphasizes that OptiTech must not only keep up with change but be a step ahead, using it as a lever for innovation and market leadership. She introduces the concept of change management frameworks and their critical role in facilitating smooth transitions.

Interactive Activities:

1. **Change Management Framework Workshops:**

- **Activity:**
- Participants are introduced to various change management models, including Kotter's 8-Step Process for Leading Change and the ADKAR model. Through group activities, they assess which model best fits OptiTech's current needs and how each can be tailored to the specifics of the AI project.
- **Impact:**
- Leaders gain insights into structured approaches to managing change, enhancing their ability to lead their teams through the transformation processes effectively.

1. **Resistance Management Training:**

- **Activity:**
- A workshop dedicated to understanding and managing resistance to change. Leaders learn about the psychological and organizational factors that cause resistance and practice strategies to engage and convert resistors into change advocates.
- **Impact:**

- This training prepares leaders to identify, anticipate, and mitigate resistance, ensuring smoother implementation of the new AI technology and other future initiatives.

1. **Role-Playing Change Scenarios:**

- **Activity:**
- Leaders participate in role-playing exercises that simulate specific challenges they might face during the AI integration. Scenarios include communicating changes to skeptical employees, managing workflow disruptions, and aligning departmental objectives with new strategic directions.
- **Impact:**
- By acting out potential problems and practicing their resolutions, leaders enhance their problem-solving and communication skills, crucial for real-world change management.

1. **Innovation and Flexibility Workshops:**

- **Activity:**
- Leaders engage in creativity and flexibility drills that challenge them to think outside the box and find innovative solutions to potential problems arising from changes. These workshops encourage thinking that is not just reactive but proactive in dealing with change.
- **Impact:**
- These sessions foster a mindset of innovation and flexibility, traits necessary for leading a technology-forward company like OptiTech.

As the seminar concludes, Elena gathers all participants to reinforce the importance of leadership in times of change. She encourages each leader to commit to being a change champion, responsible not only for implementing new processes but also for inspiring their teams to embrace these changes.

Leaders leave the seminar equipped with practical tools and frameworks to manage change effectively. They feel prepared to guide their teams through the uncertainties of the AI product launch and future innovations.

As the seminar attendees leave, energized and thoughtful, they discuss plans to apply their new skills. Elena watches them, satisfied with their readiness to embrace and lead change at OptiTech, confident that this proactive approach will ensure the company's growth and sustainability in the fast-evolving tech industry.

Understanding Change in an Organization

Following the comprehensive "Navigating Change" seminar, Elena recognizes the need to deepen OptiTech's understanding of how change impacts an organization at every level. She organizes a follow-up workshop titled "The Anatomy of Change" in a spacious conference room at OptiTech, equipped with interactive digital displays and breakout areas for small group discussions. The focus is on dissecting the layers of organizational change, from the strategic to the operational.

As OptiTech's managers and key team members fill the conference room, they find stations labeled with different aspects of organizational change: Strategy, Processes, People, and Technology. Elena, intent on ensuring that every employee understands how changes are planned and implemented across these domains, has prepared an interactive and educational day.

Elena opens the workshop with a detailed explanation of why understanding change is critical for OptiTech, especially as it stands on the brink of major technological advancements and market expansion. She emphasizes the interconnectedness of all parts of the organization and how change in one area can ripple through others.

Interactive Activities:

1. **Strategic Change Mapping:**

- **Activity:**
- Participants use digital tools to create visual maps of how strategic changes, like the introduction of new products or entry into new markets, affect various parts of the organization. They consider factors such as mission alignment, resource allocation, and market positioning.
- **Impact:**
- This mapping exercise helps employees see the big picture of strategic change and its intended outcomes, clarifying why certain decisions are made at the top level.

1. **Process Re-engineering Games:**

- **Activity:**
- Teams compete to redesign existing processes to accommodate new changes, using simulation software that models process efficiency and output quality under different scenarios.

- **Impact:**
- Engaging in process redesign helps participants understand the practical challenges and potential benefits of changing workflows and procedures to optimize performance.

1. **People and Change Role-Playing:**

- **Activity:**
- In role-playing sessions, employees act out scenarios involving training for new skills, adapting to new team structures, and managing morale during transitions. They practice communicating change effectively and providing support to their teams.
- **Impact:**
- These role-plays develop empathy and practical skills in managing human responses to change, highlighting the critical role of leadership in facilitating successful transitions.

1. **Technology Integration Demonstrations:**

- **Activity:**
- Live demonstrations show how new technologies are integrated into existing systems. Technical staff explain the steps involved, from selection and testing to rollout and troubleshooting.
- **Impact:**
- Demonstrations provide a hands-on look at the technological changes, easing concerns about new tools and showing the practical benefits of adoption.

As the workshop concludes, Elena brings everyone together for a session to integrate their learning experiences. She stresses the importance of seeing change as an opportunity for personal and organizational growth and encourages ongoing dialogue about how changes are made and managed.

Employees leave the workshop with a deeper understanding of the multifaceted nature of change within an organization. They feel more connected to OptiTech's strategic goals and more competent in their roles as agents of change.

As participants leave the room, their conversations buzz with ideas and strategies for embracing and driving change. Elena watches, pleased with the curiosity and engagement displayed throughout the day. She is confident that this deeper understanding of change will help OptiTech navigate the complexities of its industry, keeping the company agile and proactive in the face of new challenges.

Models of Change Management (Lewin, Kotter)

Buoyed by the success of the "Anatomy of Change" workshop, Elena recognizes a further educational opportunity to dive deep into the theoretical frameworks that underpin successful change management. To explore this, she sets up a strategic seminar titled "Mastering Change Models" in OptiTech's executive training room, now configured like a university classroom, complete with podiums for guest speakers, whiteboards for live illustrations, and projectors for detailed presentations.

As the OptiTech leaders gather in the transformed space, they find themselves surrounded by educational posters outlining the steps of various change models, from Lewin's simple three-step process to Kotter's more detailed eight-step change framework. Elena, committed to equipping her team with a solid theoretical understanding of how structured change can drive organizational success, has planned a detailed exploration of these models, complete with historical contexts and modern applications.

Elena begins the seminar with an insightful introduction to why mastering change management theories is crucial for leaders. She explains that understanding these models provides a blueprint for conceptualizing and implementing change effectively, which is especially critical as OptiTech prepares to roll out new technologies and strategies.

Interactive Activities:

1. **Kurt Lewin's Freeze Phases:**

- **Activity:**
- Participants engage in a group discussion led by a change management expert who explains Lewin's Freeze Phases: Unfreeze, Change, and Refreeze. They use case studies from OptiTech's past to identify instances where this model was—or could have been—effectively applied.
- **Impact:**
- This discussion helps leaders understand the psychological need to prepare an organization for change, implement new methods, and then solidify these changes into the corporate culture.

1. **John Kotter's 8-Step Process:**

- **Activity:**
- The seminar breaks down Kotter's Eight Steps for Leading Change, with each step discussed in detail through interactive workshops. Leaders analyze each step's relevance to their current roles and identify past projects where deeper knowledge of Kotter's model could have improved outcomes.
- **Impact:**
- By dissecting each step, leaders learn to appreciate the complexity and thoroughness needed in planning and executing change, especially in a tech environment where rapid innovation is standard.

1. **Model Application Labs:**

- **Activity:**
- Leaders are divided into small groups to work through a hypothetical yet plausible change scenario at OptiTech using both Lewin's and Kotter's models. They present their strategies and receive feedback from peers and experts.
- **Impact:**
- This practical application reinforces learning and allows leaders to experiment with theoretical knowledge in a risk-free setting, enhancing their confidence and skills in managing real change.

1. **Panel Discussion on Modern Adaptations:**

- **Activity:**
- A panel of industry experts discusses the evolution of

change management theories and their adaptations for modern businesses, particularly in tech sectors. They explore the integration of digital tools and social media in managing change.
- **Impact:**
- This discussion updates traditional models with contemporary practices, illustrating how foundational theories evolve to remain relevant in today's fast-paced business environment.

At the close of the seminar, Elena brings everyone together for a final reflection. She emphasizes the importance of leveraging these models not as strict guides but as flexible tools that can help navigate the complexities of change at OptiTech. She encourages leaders to continue exploring and adapting these models to fit their specific needs and challenges.

Leaders leave the seminar equipped with a deeper understanding of change management theories and practical insights into their application. They feel prepared to lead their teams through the upcoming changes with a structured approach that minimizes disruption and maximizes acceptance and effectiveness.

As the leaders depart, their thoughtful expressions and animated discussions reflect their readiness to embrace change management as a critical leadership skill. Elena watches them, reassured that with these tools, OptiTech is well-prepared to face the future, adapting and thriving in an ever-changing technological landscape.

Overcoming Resistance to Change

Following the enlightening seminar on change management models, Elena shifts focus to a crucial aspect often encountered during organizational transformation—resistance to change. Aware that the upcoming AI product launch might trigger significant resistance within OptiTech, she organizes a workshop titled "Navigating Resistance" at OptiTech's main auditorium, now equipped with virtual reality (VR) simulation areas, roundtable discussion zones, and multimedia presentations focused on strategies to overcome resistance.

As the OptiTech leaders gather in the auditorium, transformed into a dynamic learning environment, they are greeted by scenarios that simulate common resistance situations in virtual reality. Elena, determined to proactively address and dismantle barriers to change, has curated a series of activities designed to equip leaders with the skills to understand, engage with, and mitigate resistance effectively.

Elena opens the workshop with an overview of the psychological and organizational factors that often lead to resistance. She stresses the importance of empathy and communication in understanding the root causes of resistance and outlines the day's goal—to develop practical strategies that foster open dialogue and acceptance of change.

Interactive Activities:

1. **VR Resistance Scenarios:**

- **Activity:**
- Leaders don VR headsets to experience immersive simu-

lations that place them in scenarios where they face direct resistance from virtual team members. These scenarios include introducing new software tools, restructuring teams, and changing project timelines.
- **Impact:**
- This activity allows leaders to experience the emotional and practical aspects of resistance firsthand, enhancing their understanding of the employee perspective and testing their responses.

1. **Root Cause Analysis Workshops:**

- **Activity:**
- Facilitators guide leaders through root cause analysis exercises tailored to dissect past instances where OptiTech faced significant resistance. Leaders identify patterns and triggers of resistance and discuss how different approaches might have mitigated these issues.
- **Impact:**
- Understanding the underlying causes of resistance helps leaders develop more effective strategies tailored to specific concerns and fears of their teams.

1. **Communication Strategy Sessions:**

- **Activity:**
- Communication experts conduct sessions on crafting clear, empathetic, and persuasive messages intended to address concerns and highlight the benefits of change. Leaders practice delivering these messages through role-playing exercises.

- **Impact:**
- Leaders learn to communicate changes in a way that minimizes misunderstandings and builds trust, essential for reducing resistance and gaining support.

1. **Engagement and Empowerment Panels:**

- **Activity:**
- A panel of change management professionals discusses successful strategies for engaging employees and empowering them to take active roles in the change process. Topics include participatory decision-making, feedback loops, and recognition programs.
- **Impact:**
- By involving employees in the change process, leaders can transform potential resistors into change advocates, fostering a more inclusive and collaborative culture.

At the end of the workshop, Elena gathers all participants to reflect on the strategies discussed and encourages them to personalize these approaches to fit their individual teams. She emphasizes the importance of ongoing dialogue and adaptability in change management processes.

Leaders leave the workshop with a toolkit of strategies to identify, understand, and effectively manage resistance to change. They feel more confident in their ability to lead their teams through the transitions required for the AI product launch and future innovations.

As the auditorium empties, the leaders' determined strides and thoughtful expressions reflect their readiness to tackle resistance head-on. Elena watches them leave, reassured that OptiTech is better prepared to handle the challenges of change, with leaders who are not only capable of managing resistance but are equipped to transform it into constructive engagement.

Role of Change Agents

After addressing resistance to change, Elena realizes the need to empower specific individuals within OptiTech who can act as catalysts for change—Change Agents. To cultivate and support these key figures, she organizes an intensive training program titled "Empowering Change Agents" at a serene retreat location outside the city. The venue is chosen for its calming environment, which fosters open-mindedness and creativity, and is equipped with collaborative workspaces, technology-enhanced training rooms, and outdoor team-building areas.

As OptiTech's potential change agents arrive at the retreat, they are welcomed into a space that blends natural beauty with modern training facilities. Elena, committed to developing a robust network of skilled change agents who can lead by example and guide their peers through the transformation processes, has devised a program rich in educational content, practical exercises, and leadership development activities.

Elena begins the training program with an inspiring talk about the critical role of change agents in the success of organizational transformations. She explains that change agents are not just implementers of change but also visionaries who inspire, motivate, and support their colleagues. She outlines the expectations for these roles and the skills the training will focus on developing.

Interactive Activities:

1. **Skills Development Workshops:**

- **Activity:**
- Expert facilitators conduct workshops on key skills for change agents, including strategic thinking, effective communication, empathy, and resilience. Participants engage in interactive exercises that challenge them to use these skills in hypothetical change scenarios.
- **Impact:**
- These workshops are designed to equip change agents with the necessary competencies to handle uncertainties and to lead change initiatives confidently and competently.

1. **Role-Playing Leadership Challenges:**

- **Activity:**
- In role-playing sessions, participants face various leadership challenges that test their ability to apply their new skills in real-world-like situations. These include handling resistance, communicating change benefits to skeptical employees, and maintaining team morale.
- **Impact:**
- Role-playing helps change agents experience the dynamics of leading change firsthand, providing them with insights into the practical challenges and best practices for overcoming them.

1. **Mentorship Program Kickoff:**

- **Activity:**
- Elena introduces a mentorship program where experienced leaders at OptiTech pair up with change agents to provide guidance, support, and feedback throughout the implementation of change projects.
- **Impact:**
- The mentorship program ensures that change agents have ongoing support and a resource for advice, helping them to continually develop their leadership skills and effectiveness.

1. **Collaborative Strategy Sessions:**

- **Activity:**
- Participants work in groups to create detailed action plans for upcoming change initiatives, including the AI product launch. These plans include specific goals, timelines, resource allocations, and contingency strategies.
- **Impact:**
- Collaborative planning not only solidifies the learning outcomes of the training program but also prepares change agents to take active, informed roles in leading change at OptiTech.

As the training program concludes, Elena gathers all participants to celebrate their completion of the course and to discuss their commitments as change agents. She emphasizes the importance of their leadership in the success of OptiTech's future and expresses her confidence in their ability to inspire and lead their teams.

Participants leave the retreat with a clear understanding

of their roles as change agents, equipped with the tools, strategies, and support needed to drive effective change. They feel empowered and ready to act as both leaders and facilitators in transforming OptiTech's operational and cultural landscape.

As the newly trained change agents depart, energized and equipped with new insights and skills, Elena feels a profound sense of optimism. She watches them leave, knowing that these individuals will play crucial roles in steering OptiTech through upcoming changes and beyond, ensuring the company remains at the forefront of innovation and market leadership.

Strategies for Successful Change Implementation

After empowering a network of change agents, Elena realizes the importance of equipping them with specific, actionable strategies to ensure successful change implementation. To address this, she organizes a strategic workshop titled "Blueprints for Change" within OptiTech's innovation hub. The venue is set up with collaboration zones, tech-enabled discussion tables, and areas dedicated to strategy development, all designed to facilitate a hands-on approach to planning and execution.

As OptiTech's change agents gather in the innovation hub, they find a dynamic environment waiting for them, complete with digital boards for mapping strategies and tools for real-time feedback and simulation. Elena, determined to see OptiTech through a successful transition with the upcoming AI product launch and other key initiatives, has prepared a comprehensive program focused on translating change theory into practical, effective actions.

Elena starts the workshop with a motivating speech about the power of well-planned and well-executed change. She emphasizes that the strategies developed today will directly impact the success of OptiTech's ambitious projects. She outlines the key areas of focus: communication planning, stakeholder engagement, resource allocation, and monitoring and evaluation.

Interactive Activities:

1. **Communication Strategy Development:**

- **Activity:**
- Change agents participate in a workshop to develop detailed communication plans that outline how changes will be communicated to different segments of the organization. They use interactive software to customize messages according to department, role, and location.
- **Impact:**
- Tailored communication strategies ensure that all employees understand why change is happening, what it entails, and how it will benefit them, thereby reducing resistance and fostering a supportive environment.

1. **Stakeholder Engagement Sessions:**

- **Activity:**
- Through role-playing exercises, change agents practice engaging with different stakeholders, including skeptical or resistant groups. They work on negotiation skills,

empathy, and strategies to gain buy-in.
- **Impact:**
- Engaging effectively with stakeholders strengthens the support base for the change initiatives and identifies potential champions who can influence others.

1. **Resource Allocation Workshops:**

- **Activity:**
- Participants use simulations to allocate resources for change initiatives effectively. They consider factors like budget constraints, human resources needs, and timelines, ensuring that all projects have the necessary support to succeed.
- **Impact:**
- Proper resource allocation prevents overstretching and ensures that each phase of the change process is well-supported, increasing the likelihood of success.

1. **Monitoring and Evaluation Planning:**

- **Activity:**
- Change agents develop monitoring and evaluation plans that include key performance indicators, feedback mechanisms, and regular review points. This session focuses on creating adaptable strategies that can respond to ongoing findings.
- **Impact:**
- Continuous monitoring and evaluation enable the change team to track progress, celebrate milestones, adjust strategies as needed, and demonstrate the impact of

changes to the entire organization.

As the workshop concludes, Elena brings everyone together to reinforce the commitment to these strategies. She stresses the importance of agility and continuous learning, encouraging change agents to remain adaptable and responsive as they roll out changes.

Leaders leave the workshop with a robust set of strategies tailored to facilitate successful change within OptiTech. They feel prepared, supported, and confident in their ability to lead the company through its transformative journey.

Watching her team collaborate and innovate with renewed energy and focus, Elena feels a deep sense of satisfaction and optimism. She knows that with these strategies in place, OptiTech is well-equipped to implement change not just effectively but in a way that aligns with its core values and long-term vision.

Evaluating Change Effectiveness

After empowering her change agents and setting strategic plans into motion, Elena recognizes the necessity of evaluating the effectiveness of these changes to ensure they meet OptiTech's ambitious goals. To systematically approach this critical task, she organizes a seminar titled "Measuring Impact: Evaluating Change Effectiveness" at OptiTech's headquarters, transforming a large conference room into a data-driven analysis center complete with advanced analytics tools, interactive dashboards, and areas for deep-dive sessions into specific change initiatives.

As OptiTech's leaders and change agents convene in the

data-centric setup, they are greeted by a network of screens displaying real-time data from ongoing change projects. Elena, determined to instill a culture of accountability and continuous improvement, has prepared a detailed agenda that focuses on data interpretation, success metrics, and iterative strategy adjustments.

Elena begins the seminar with a discussion on the importance of outcome-based evaluation in change management. She highlights that effective evaluation is not just about tracking timelines and budget adherence but also measuring the broader impact on company performance, employee satisfaction, and market position.

Interactive Activities:

1. **Key Performance Indicator (KPI) Workshop:**

- **Activity:**
- Leaders participate in workshops to identify and refine the key performance indicators for each major change initiative. These KPIs range from quantitative metrics like sales figures and market share to qualitative indicators such as employee engagement and customer satisfaction.
- **Impact:**
- This workshop helps leaders understand how to effectively measure what matters most to the success of each change initiative, ensuring that the KPIs are aligned with OptiTech's strategic objectives.

1. **Data Analytics Training:**

- **Activity:**
- A session led by data scientists who introduce the latest tools and methodologies for analyzing change-related data. Participants learn how to use data visualization tools to interpret complex data sets and extract actionable insights.
- **Impact:**
- Equipping leaders with data analytics skills enables them to independently assess and understand the impact of changes, fostering a data-driven approach to decision-making.

1. **Roundtable Discussion on Challenges and Adjustments:**

- **Activity:**
- Leaders share their experiences and challenges encountered during the implementation of changes. This roundtable provides a platform for collaborative problem-solving, where leaders propose adjustments and improvements to current strategies based on their firsthand experiences and data insights.
- **Impact:**
- This discussion not only fosters a sense of community among leaders but also promotes the sharing of best practices and lessons learned, crucial for refining change strategies.

1. **Feedback Integration Session:**

- **Activity:**

- A feedback integration session where employees from various levels of the organization provide input on how the changes have affected their work and well-being. This session uses anonymous feedback tools and live surveys to gather honest and comprehensive feedback.
- **Impact:**
- Direct feedback from employees helps leaders gauge the real impact of the changes, highlighting areas where expectations may not align with reality and where additional support may be required.

As the seminar concludes, Elena emphasizes the importance of staying responsive to the data and feedback collected. She encourages leaders to view evaluation as an ongoing process that doesn't end with the implementation of changes but is a key component of sustainable growth and adaptation.

Leaders leave the seminar equipped with the tools and knowledge to measure the effectiveness of changes accurately and make informed decisions about future directions. They feel empowered to take ownership of their projects, with a clear understanding of how to align their actions with broader organizational goals.

As the participants disperse, their animated discussions about data and strategies echo through the halls. Elena watches them, reassured that OptiTech is cultivating a robust framework for change management that not only adapts to the present but is also scalable for future challenges.

12

Chapter 12: Technology and Innovation

With OptiTech's new AI product nearing launch and the organization now adept in managing change, Elena turns her focus towards sustaining long-term innovation and integrating cutting-edge technology. She organizes a visionary event titled "Future Horizons: Technology and Innovation at OptiTech," hosted in a newly inaugurated Innovation Lab, designed with futuristic architecture and equipped with the latest in immersive technology and interactive displays.

As OptiTech's leaders and top innovators gather in the strikingly modern Innovation Lab, they find themselves surrounded by interactive tech installations showcasing everything from AI-driven analytics to virtual reality workspaces. Elena, determined to keep OptiTech at the forefront of technological advancement, has planned a dynamic program to explore emerging technologies and foster a culture of continuous innovation.

Elena opens the event with a powerful message about

the importance of staying ahead in a rapidly evolving tech landscape. She discusses the pivotal role of embracing new technologies not just for competitive advantage but also for driving societal progress. She outlines the sessions designed to spark creativity and initiative among the team.

Interactive Activities:

1. **Tech Demos and Interactive Sessions:**

   - **Activity:**
   - Participants explore various technology stations, each demonstrating a new tool or platform. These range from AI algorithms that predict market trends to VR systems for remote collaboration.
   - **Impact:**
   - Experiencing these technologies firsthand not only ignites interest but also provides practical insights into how these tools can be leveraged within OptiTech's projects and processes.

1. **Innovation Workshops:**

   - **Activity:**
   - Facilitated by leading tech innovators and thinkers, these workshops challenge participants to brainstorm applications for emerging technologies in their fields. Workshops focus on ideation, rapid prototyping, and user-centric design principles.
   - **Impact:**
   - Leaders and innovators are encouraged to think beyond

conventional boundaries, fostering a proactive approach to innovation that anticipates future challenges and opportunities.

1. **Panel Discussion on Technology Ethics:**

- **Activity:**
- A diverse panel of ethicists, tech leaders, and regulatory experts discuss the ethical considerations of deploying new technologies, particularly AI. Topics include privacy, bias in machine learning, and the impact of automation on employment.
- **Impact:**
- This critical conversation ensures that OptiTech's commitment to innovation is balanced with ethical considerations, promoting responsible development and application of technology.

1. **Future Trend Analysis Sessions:**

- **Activity:**
- Experts in tech trend analysis present data and forecasts on the next big waves in technology. Participants use this information to assess potential impacts on their strategic plans and to identify areas for early investment or development.
- **Impact:**
- By staying informed on future trends, OptiTech can better position itself as a leader in technology and innovation, ensuring readiness and adaptability.

As the event concludes, Elena gathers feedback on the sessions and discusses how these insights can be integrated into OptiTech's long-term strategies. She reiterates her commitment to investing in the tools, talent, and training necessary to lead in innovation.

Leaders and innovators leave the event inspired and equipped with the knowledge and tools to drive forward-thinking projects. They appreciate the significance of integrating advanced technology not just in their products but across their operational processes.

As the crowd disperses, the energy in the Innovation Lab is palpable, with conversations buzzing about new ideas and collaborative possibilities. Elena watches contentedly, confident that OptiTech is well-prepared to continue its legacy of innovation and excellence, shaping the future of technology while addressing the needs and challenges of tomorrow.

Impact of Technology on Organizational Behavior

Following the stimulating "Future Horizons" event, Elena decides to delve deeper into how technology specifically affects organizational behavior at OptiTech. To facilitate this important exploration, she organizes a targeted workshop titled "Techfluence: The Impact of Technology on Organizational Behavior" at OptiTech's R&D center. The center is equipped with behavioral analytics tools, collaboration software demonstrations, and spaces designed for interactive learning and real-time feedback on technology use.

As OptiTech's diverse teams, including engineers, HR professionals, and managers, enter the R&D center, they encounter a variety of stations each showcasing different technological tools and their influence on workplace dynamics, communication, and productivity. Elena, keen to foster a deeper understanding of the interplay between technology and employee behavior, has prepared a day filled with activities that not only inform but also engage participants in critical thinking about the future of work at OptiTech.

Elena begins the workshop with an overview of recent technological advancements within OptiTech and their broader implications for organizational behavior. She emphasizes the dual role of technology as both a facilitator and a disruptor in the workplace, setting the stage for a day dedicated to unpacking these dynamics.

Interactive Activities:

1. **Behavioral Analytics Demonstrations:**

- **Activity:**
- Participants explore real-time data from behavioral analytics software that monitors and analyzes employee interactions, workflows, and productivity patterns in different scenarios, both with and without specific technological tools.
- **Impact:**
- These demonstrations help visualize how technology alters workplace behaviors, highlighting both positive impacts on efficiency and potential challenges such as over-reliance or miscommunication.

1. **Collaboration Technology Trials:**

- **Activity:**
- Teams engage in hands-on trials of various collaboration platforms and communication tools designed to enhance connectivity in remote and hybrid work settings. Participants assess these technologies' effectiveness in facilitating teamwork and maintaining corporate culture.
- **Impact:**
- By directly experiencing these tools, participants gain insights into how technology can enhance or hinder collaboration and what adjustments may be necessary to optimize team dynamics.

1. **Roundtable Discussions on Technology and Ethics:**

- **Activity:**
- A roundtable discussion focuses on the ethical considerations of using advanced technologies in the workplace, such as surveillance tools, AI in hiring practices, and algorithm-driven decision-making.
- **Impact:**
- These discussions raise awareness about the ethical implications of technological adoption, prompting a broader conversation about maintaining transparency, fairness, and respect for privacy.

1. **Future of Work Strategy Sessions:**

- **Activity:**
- In these strategy sessions, leaders and employees work

together to outline future scenarios impacted by new technologies. They develop potential guidelines and policies that balance technological efficiencies with employee well-being and organizational culture.
- **Impact:**
- These sessions help participants proactively plan for changes in organizational behavior driven by technology, ensuring that OptiTech remains a forward-thinking, employee-centered workplace.

As the workshop concludes, Elena encourages everyone to continue reflecting on and discussing the day's findings. She emphasizes the importance of being adaptive and informed as technology continues to evolve, and the need for policies that ensure technological impacts on organizational behavior are positive and inclusive.

Participants leave the workshop with a nuanced understanding of how technology influences organizational behavior at multiple levels. They are equipped with the knowledge to help guide the integration of new technologies in ways that strengthen rather than disrupt OptiTech's operational and cultural fabric.

As the participants leave the R&D center, their discussions are rich with ideas and concerns about the future integration of technology in the workplace. Elena watches with a sense of accomplishment, knowing that these conversations are crucial for shaping a technology-informed yet human-centered organizational strategy at OptiTech.

Managing Technological Change

Following the deep dive into how technology impacts organizational behavior, Elena shifts focus to the management aspects of technological change. Recognizing that the successful launch of the AI product and subsequent technological updates will require precise management strategies, she organizes a capstone seminar titled "Mastering Technological Change" in OptiTech's state-of-the-art conference facility. The setup includes simulation labs for testing change management theories, augmented reality (AR) stations for scenario-based learning, and discussion pods for collaborative strategy development.

As OptiTech's senior executives, project managers, and IT specialists convene, they are met with an environment that mirrors the cutting edge of their industry. Interactive stations around the room offer hands-on experiences with the latest change management software and tools, while AR stations provide immersive learning experiences about potential future scenarios. Elena, committed to ensuring that technological change is seamlessly integrated into OptiTech's operations, has planned a comprehensive curriculum that covers everything from initial adoption to full-scale implementation.

Elena begins the seminar with a keynote on the dual nature of technology as both an enabler and a disruptor. She outlines the essential management strategies that will be explored during the seminar, emphasizing that the goal is to equip leaders with the skills to not only manage but also capitalize on technological change.

Interactive Activities:

1. **Adoption Strategy Workshops:**

- **Activity:**
- Leaders participate in workshops focused on developing adoption strategies that minimize disruption while maximizing engagement. These sessions include the analysis of past technology rollouts at OptiTech, identifying what worked and what didn't.
- **Impact:**
- Participants refine their approaches to technology adoption, ensuring that new technologies are embraced company-wide, enhancing efficiency and productivity.

1. **AR Scenario Planning:**

- **Activity:**
- In AR-driven scenarios, participants face various challenges related to technological implementation, from budget overruns to employee resistance, and must navigate these hurdles successfully.
- **Impact:**
- This hands-on experience with potential real-world problems prepares leaders to think on their feet and adapt strategies dynamically, a crucial skill in technology management.

1. **Change Management Simulations:**

- **Activity:**

- Using advanced simulations, leaders practice implementing large-scale technological changes, applying different models and tools discussed in previous workshops to monitor outcomes and adjust tactics in real time.
- **Impact:**
- Simulations provide a risk-free environment to test change management strategies, helping leaders gain confidence in their ability to handle complex technology transitions.

1. **Roundtable Discussions on Sustainable Practices:**

- **Activity:**
- Leaders engage in roundtable discussions about maintaining sustainability during technological upgrades, including considerations of environmental impact, ethical use of technology, and long-term scalability.
- **Impact:**
- These discussions emphasize the importance of considering broader impacts when integrating new technologies, aligning OptiTech's technological advancements with its corporate social responsibility goals.

At the conclusion of the seminar, Elena gathers all participants to emphasize the importance of leadership in technological change. She challenges them to apply what they've learned not only to the upcoming AI product launch but to all future technological initiatives at OptiTech.

Leaders leave the seminar equipped with a robust toolkit for managing technological change, understanding the importance of strategic planning, employee engagement, and continuous evaluation.

As they leave the conference facility, OptiTech's leaders are not just prepared; they are motivated to guide their teams through the complexities of technological evolution. Elena watches them go, confident in their abilities to drive OptiTech towards a technologically advanced future, ready to meet the next wave of industry innovations head-on.

Fostering an Innovative Culture

After establishing frameworks for managing technological change, Elena recognizes that fostering a culture that inherently supports innovation is crucial for sustained growth and competitiveness. Inspired to embed this culture deeply within OptiTech, she organizes a transformative retreat called "Innovate OptiTech" at a scenic, secluded resort. The environment is designed to break away from traditional corporate settings and stimulate creativity, featuring workshops in open-air tents, brainstorming sessions by the lake, and innovation challenges in nature-inspired think tanks.

As OptiTech's leaders and key creative teams arrive at the resort, they are greeted by an atmosphere that breathes innovation. Each element of the retreat is carefully crafted to encourage free thinking and spontaneous collaboration. Elena, determined to cultivate a mindset that views challenges as opportunities for innovation, has planned a series of activities that not only inspire new ideas but also create actionable plans to integrate these ideas into OptiTech's operational fabric.

Elena begins the retreat with an energizing talk about the power of innovation in driving technological and market leadership. She shares stories of past industry disruptions led by innovative thinking and sets the stage for a retreat focused on embedding such thinking into every layer of OptiTech.

Interactive Activities:

1. **Creative Workshops:**

- **Activity:**
- Facilitators lead creative problem-solving workshops that challenge participants to think outside the box and develop novel solutions to hypothetical business challenges. These workshops use techniques like design thinking, reverse brainstorming, and SCAMPER.
- **Impact:**
- These creative exercises stimulate unconventional thinking and demonstrate how a shift in perspective can lead to breakthrough ideas in technology and business processes.

1. **Innovation Challenges:**

- **Activity:**
- Teams compete in innovation challenges that require them to use limited resources to build prototypes that solve real-world problems related to OptiTech's market. Challenges are judged on creativity, feasibility, and potential impact.
- **Impact:**
- Engaging in hands-on innovation under competitive conditions energizes teams and fosters a can-do spirit that is essential for a culture of innovation.

1. **Technology Exploration Zones:**

- **Activity:**
- Participants explore technology exploration zones equipped with the latest tech gadgets, software tools, and emerging technologies like AR and AI. Experts are on hand to discuss the potential applications of these technologies in OptiTech's operations.
- **Impact:**
- Exposure to cutting-edge technologies encourages staff to think about how these can be harnessed to enhance OptiTech's products and services, keeping the company at the forefront of technological advancements.

1. **Cultural Shift Workshops:**

- **Activity:**
- Leaders attend workshops focused on strategies for leading cultural change towards sustained innovation. Topics include creating safe spaces for risk-taking, rewarding innovation, and integrating new ideas into existing business models.
- **Impact:**
- These sessions provide leaders with practical tools and strategies to nurture and sustain a culture that celebrates and drives innovation at all levels of the organization.

As the retreat concludes, Elena gathers feedback on the initiatives and discussions. She emphasizes the ongoing commitment required to maintain a culture of innovation, encouraging everyone to take ownership of this endeavor.

She outlines follow-up steps that include the establishment of an innovation advisory board and regular innovation audits.

Participants leave the retreat invigorated with a new appreciation for the role of creativity and innovation in OptiTech's success. They return to work equipped with fresh ideas and a new mindset ready to embrace and drive change.

As the retreat ends and participants slowly depart from the serene setting, the buzz of inspired conversation and laughter fills the air. Elena watches on, confident that the seeds of a lasting innovative culture have been sown, ready to propel OptiTech into a future where innovation is not just an output but the core of its identity.

Challenges of Innovation in Large Organizations

Having successfully ignited a spirit of innovation across OptiTech with the "Innovate OptiTech" retreat, Elena turns her attention to the realistic challenges that large organizations like hers often face when trying to sustain innovation. To address these, she organizes a follow-up seminar titled "Navigating Innovation Challenges in Large Organizations" back at OptiTech headquarters, transforming a large conference room into a series of breakout areas each themed around specific innovation challenges.

As OptiTech's department heads and innovation team leads gather, they find themselves surrounded by interactive displays that depict various scenarios highlighting the typical hurdles in sustaining innovation within a large corporate structure. Elena, keen to foster not just temporary enthusiasm but lasting capability, has curated a series of panels, workshops, and strategy sessions focused on identifying, understanding, and overcoming these barriers.

Elena opens the seminar with a compelling overview of the paradox that large organizations face: the need to innovate against the innate resistance to change. She outlines the primary challenges—structural inertia, risk aversion, and process rigidity—and how these can stifle innovation if not proactively managed.

Interactive Activities:

1. **Panel Discussion on Structural Inertia:**

- **Activity:**
- A panel of external business leaders who have successfully overcome structural inertia shares their experiences and strategies. They discuss how to reshape organizational structures to be more conducive to innovation.
- **Impact:**
- These insights help OptiTech's leaders understand practical measures to minimize bureaucratic slowdowns and enhance flexibility within their existing structures.

1. **Workshop on Cultivating Risk-Tolerance:**

- **Activity:**
- Through guided workshops, participants explore techniques to foster a culture that not only tolerates but encourages calculated risks. This includes the use of failure as a learning tool and the creation of 'safe fail' projects.
- **Impact:**

- Leaders learn how to create an environment where risk is not shunned but is seen as a necessary element of innovation, thereby fostering a more dynamic approach to new initiatives.

1. **Breakout Sessions on Streamlining Processes:**

- **Activity:**
- In breakout sessions, leaders tackle the challenge of process rigidity by redesigning workflows to allow greater creativity and faster execution. Participants use real OptiTech processes as case studies for potential simplification and agility enhancement.
- **Impact:**
- These sessions provide tangible solutions that participants can implement to reduce procedural bottlenecks and empower quicker decision-making and project launches.

1. **Strategy Roundtables on Innovation Metrics:**

- **Activity:**
- Leaders participate in roundtables to develop new metrics that more accurately reflect the value of innovation efforts beyond immediate financial returns. This involves integrating innovation metrics into performance evaluations and corporate dashboards.
- **Impact:**
- By redefining how success is measured, OptiTech can ensure that its innovation efforts are not only recognized but also directly tied to the company's strategic goals and

employee performance evaluations.

As the seminar concludes, Elena facilitates a closing discussion that encourages leaders to share their commitments to implementing the strategies discussed. She emphasizes the importance of leadership buy-in and continuous reassessment as key to overcoming innovation challenges in a large organization.

Leaders leave the seminar equipped with specific strategies and a deeper understanding of the systemic changes needed to foster ongoing innovation at OptiTech. They feel empowered to initiate practical changes that will facilitate a more innovative corporate culture.

As the participants disperse, there's a palpable sense of purpose and determination among them. Elena watches with satisfaction, confident that these leaders are now better prepared to turn the tide against the inherent challenges of innovation in a large organization, steering OptiTech towards a future where innovation is both celebrated and systematically cultivated.

Role of Social Media and Digital Platforms

With OptiTech's leadership now well-versed in the complexities of fostering innovation within a large organization, Elena recognizes the potential of leveraging modern digital tools to further these goals. To harness this potential, she organizes a forward-thinking workshop titled "Digital Horizons: Leveraging Social Media and Digital Platforms for Innovation" at OptiTech's digital media center. The center is transformed into a high-tech arena, featuring live demos of cutting-edge social media tools, interactive digital stations, and areas for collaborative digital content creation.

As OptiTech's marketing, R&D, and IT teams gather in the digitally charged setting, they find themselves surrounded by screens displaying real-time data feeds, social media analytics, and examples of digital content that have driven innovation in various industries. Elena, keen to integrate these tools into OptiTech's innovation strategy, has planned a day filled with hands-on activities and expert-led sessions designed to explore the expansive role of digital platforms in driving technological advancement and engaging with wider communities.

Elena starts the workshop with an engaging overview of the digital landscape, emphasizing how platforms like Twitter, LinkedIn, and specialized industry forums have transformed the way organizations innovate and interact with their customers and peers. She outlines the key benefits of these tools, including market intelligence, customer feedback, and enhanced collaborative opportunities.

Interactive Activities:

1. **Social Media Strategy Sprint:**

- **Activity:**
- In a fast-paced strategy sprint, participants form teams to create mock social media campaigns that promote new OptiTech innovations. They use real-time feedback tools to measure the potential effectiveness and engagement level of their campaigns.
- **Impact:**

- This exercise allows participants to practically apply their ideas in a controlled environment, learning how to effectively use social media to generate buzz and foster community engagement around innovation.

1. **Digital Collaboration Workshops:**

- **Activity:**
- Experts in digital collaboration platforms conduct workshops on leveraging these tools to enhance internal collaboration. Participants learn about the latest in project management software, communication apps, and collaborative innovation platforms like Slack, Trello, and Microsoft Teams.
- **Impact:**
- Participants explore new ways to enhance productivity and streamline communication across departments, crucial for accelerating the innovation process at OptiTech.

1. **Panel Discussion on Digital Ethics:**

- **Activity:**
- A panel of digital ethics experts discusses the challenges and responsibilities associated with using social media and digital platforms, particularly issues related to data privacy, misinformation, and digital footprint management.
- **Impact:**
- This discussion raises awareness about the ethical considerations of digital engagements and helps formulate policies that ensure responsible use of these powerful

tools.

1. **Influencer Engagement Simulation:**

- **Activity:**
- Teams engage in a simulation where they must collaborate with digital influencers to promote technological innovations. The simulation includes negotiating partnerships, content co-creation, and measuring the impact of influencer engagement.
- **Impact:**
- This activity provides insights into the world of digital marketing and influencer partnerships, offering strategies to extend OptiTech's reach and influence in the digital space.

As the workshop concludes, Elena brings everyone together to reflect on the insights gained and the practical applications of the tools explored. She emphasizes the importance of integrating digital strategies into OptiTech's broader innovation efforts and encourages ongoing experimentation and learning.

Participants leave the workshop equipped with new skills and strategies to leverage social media and digital platforms effectively. They feel empowered to integrate these tools into their daily operations and long-term innovation strategies.

As the participants leave the digital media center, their conversations buzz with ideas for new digital projects and strategies. Elena watches them depart, satisfied with the knowledge that OptiTech is poised to enhance its innovative capabilities and market presence through the strategic use of digital platforms.

Future Trends in Workplace Technology

After exploring the integration of social media and digital platforms at OptiTech, Elena decides to shift her focus towards preparing for the future by addressing upcoming trends in workplace technology. To showcase and explore these trends, she organizes a visionary conference titled "Tomorrow's Tech Today" at OptiTech's newly designed Innovation Hub, which is equipped with the latest augmented reality (AR) and virtual reality (VR) setups, smart office solutions, and AI-driven analytics systems.

As OptiTech's executives, technology officers, and innovation teams arrive at the Innovation Hub, they are greeted by an immersive experience that feels like stepping into the future. Interactive displays and live demonstrations of emerging technologies such as AI assistants, IoT-connected workplace tools, and next-generation cybersecurity systems fill the space. Elena, committed to keeping OptiTech at the cutting edge, has arranged for industry leaders and tech innovators to present and discuss these technologies.

Elena begins the conference with an inspiring talk about the velocity of technological change and its profound implications for the workplace. She emphasizes the importance of not only adapting to but anticipating and shaping these changes to maintain OptiTech's leadership in the tech industry.

Interactive Activities:

1. **AR and VR Demonstrations:**

- **Activity:**
- Participants explore AR and VR stations that simulate future workplace environments, including virtual meetings spaces that mimic physical presence, and training modules that use VR for skills development.
- **Impact:**
- These demonstrations provide a tangible look at how emerging technologies can enhance collaboration and training, offering a more engaging and effective workplace experience.

1. **Panel Discussion on AI in the Workplace:**

- **Activity:**
- A panel of AI experts discusses the future role of artificial intelligence in the workplace, focusing on automation, data analysis, and decision-making processes. The discussion covers the benefits and challenges, including the ethical implications and the need for new skills development.
- **Impact:**
- This panel helps participants understand the strategic importance of AI and prepares them for the integration challenges and opportunities AI presents.

1. **IoT Connectivity Workshops:**

- **Activity:**
- Workshops on the Internet of Things (IoT) showcase how connectivity can be enhanced within the workplace, demonstrating smart office devices that optimize everything from energy use to employee health monitoring.
- **Impact:**
- Participants learn how IoT can create a more responsive and efficient work environment, reducing costs and improving employee well-being.

1. **Cybersecurity Breakout Sessions:**

- **Activity:**
- Given the rise of digital technologies, cybersecurity breakout sessions provide critical insights into protecting sensitive information and maintaining trust in an increasingly connected and technologically driven workplace.
- **Impact:**
- These sessions highlight the growing importance of cybersecurity measures, equipping participants with knowledge to safeguard their future workplaces effectively.

At the close of the conference, Elena gathers feedback from the participants and discusses the steps OptiTech will take to integrate these technologies responsibly and innovatively. She highlights the need for ongoing education and flexibility as tech evolves and stresses OptiTech's commitment to being at the forefront of these changes.

Leaders and innovators leave the conference with a robust understanding of how future technologies will shape the workplace. They are inspired by the potential of these tools to transform OptiTech's operations and are eager to begin integrating them into their strategic planning.

As the participants depart, their animated discussions about potential applications of the day's technologies reflect a shared excitement for the future. Elena watches on, confident that OptiTech is well-prepared to lead in a future where technology continuously redefines the workplace, driving innovation and efficiency to new heights.

13

Chapter 13: Ethics and Corporate Social Responsibility

With OptiTech navigating the waters of rapid technological innovation and expansion, Elena becomes increasingly aware of the need to anchor these advancements within a strong ethical framework and a commitment to corporate social responsibility (CSR). To address these crucial aspects, she organizes a significant summit called "Ethics in Innovation: Building a Sustainable Future" at OptiTech's headquarters, transforming the main hall into a forum for dialogue on ethical practices and CSR initiatives.

As OptiTech's employees from various departments gather, the venue buzzes with anticipation. Displays around the room highlight OptiTech's past CSR activities and commitments to ethical practices, setting the stage for a day dedicated to reinforcing these values in the company's culture. Elena, committed to ensuring that OptiTech not only leads in innovation but also in ethical business practices, has arranged for ethics experts, environmental advocates, and community leaders to speak and conduct workshops.

Elena opens the summit with a powerful call to ethical action, emphasizing that true innovation must consider its impact on society and the environment. She discusses the importance of integrating ethical decision-making into every aspect of OptiTech's operations and outlines the goals for the summit—to enhance understanding of ethical challenges in technology and to foster a culture that prioritizes CSR across all projects.

Interactive Activities:

1. **Ethics Workshops:**

- **Activity:**
- Led by renowned ethicists and business leaders, these workshops explore real-world scenarios that challenge participants to navigate complex ethical dilemmas involving data privacy, AI ethics, and equitable technology deployment.
- **Impact:**
- Participants gain practical insights into making ethical decisions that align with OptiTech's core values and the broader expectations of society.

1. **Sustainability Panels:**

- **Activity:**
- Panels discuss the environmental impact of technological products and services, featuring speakers from environmental NGOs and sustainability experts who provide

insights into eco-friendly practices.
- **Impact:**
- These discussions highlight the importance of sustainable operations and inspire employees to develop greener solutions in their projects.

1. **Community Engagement Breakout Sessions:**

- **Activity:**
- Breakout sessions focus on enhancing community engagement and contributions. Employees brainstorm initiatives that leverage OptiTech's technological resources to benefit local communities, focusing on education, healthcare, and economic development.
- **Impact:**
- These sessions help cultivate a sense of social responsibility, encouraging teams to design projects that give back to the community.

1. **CSR Strategy Roundtables:**

- **Activity:**
- Roundtables are conducted to review and strengthen OptiTech's CSR strategies. Participants evaluate current initiatives' effectiveness and discuss new proposals that align with the company's growth and ethical commitments.
- **Impact:**
- Employees take an active role in shaping the company's CSR efforts, ensuring these strategies are robust, impactful, and integrated with the company's overall goals.

As the summit concludes, Elena brings everyone together to reflect on the day's lessons and discussions. She emphasizes the critical role each employee plays in upholding OptiTech's ethical standards and advancing its CSR goals. She encourages ongoing education, vigilance, and a proactive approach to incorporating these principles into daily work and corporate policy.

Participants leave the summit with a reinforced understanding of the importance of ethics and corporate social responsibility in sustaining business success and societal well-being. They feel empowered and responsible for championing these principles within their roles at OptiTech.

As the summit attendees disperse, their conversations are rich with ideas for new CSR projects and ethical guidelines. Elena watches with pride and optimism, knowing that OptiTech is well on its path to being recognized not just for its technological prowess but also as a leader in ethical business practices and social responsibility.

Importance of Ethics in Organizational Behavior

Following the impactful "Ethics in Innovation: Building a Sustainable Future" summit, Elena decides to delve deeper into how ethics directly influence organizational behavior at OptiTech. To explore this critical aspect, she organizes a series of interactive seminars titled "Ethical Foundations in Organizational Behavior" held in the main auditorium at OptiTech, which has been set up with discussion circles, ethical dilemma simulation stations, and a central stage for keynote speakers.

As OptiTech's diverse workforce, including team leaders,

managers, and new hires, gathers in the auditorium, they find themselves in an environment designed to foster open dialogue and critical thinking about ethics. The setup encourages participation and reflection on how individual and collective behavior within the organization can align with broader ethical standards. Elena, committed to embedding a strong ethical culture at OptiTech, has prepared a curriculum that includes case studies, ethical decision-making workshops, and guest lectures from leading ethicists.

Elena opens the seminar with a compelling speech about the foundational role of ethics in shaping organizational culture and behavior. She stresses that ethical behavior is not just about compliance with laws and regulations but is a cornerstone of trust, credibility, and long-term success in business.

Interactive Activities:

1. **Ethical Dilemma Workshops:**

- **Activity:**
- Participants engage in workshops where they are presented with hypothetical scenarios involving ethical dilemmas similar to those they might face at OptiTech. These include issues like data privacy, conflicts of interest, and pressures to compromise on quality or safety for cost savings.
- **Impact:**
- Through role-play and group discussions, employees explore various outcomes based on different ethical choices, enhancing their understanding of the consequences of

decisions and actions.

1. **Keynote Series on Ethics in Tech:**

- **Activity:**
- Renowned ethicists and business leaders specializing in technology ethics deliver talks on the importance of maintaining ethical standards in the face of rapid technological advancements and competitive pressures.
- **Impact:**
- These talks provide insights into best practices for integrating ethical considerations into daily operations and long-term strategic planning, reinforcing the message that ethical behavior drives sustainable innovation.

1. **Panel Discussions on Real-World Ethical Challenges:**

- **Activity:**
- A panel featuring senior OptiTech employees who have navigated ethical challenges shares their experiences and the lessons learned. These discussions are followed by Q&A sessions where employees can ask questions and seek advice on ethical issues.
- **Impact:**
- Hearing firsthand from colleagues helps demystify ethics in the workplace and encourages employees to seek guidance and speak up when faced with ethical challenges.

1. **Ethics and Leadership Roundtables:**

CHAPTER 13: ETHICS AND CORPORATE SOCIAL RESPONSIBILITY

- **Activity:**
- In these roundtable sessions, leaders from various departments discuss how to foster an ethical climate within their teams. Topics include setting clear ethical expectations, modeling desired behaviors, and creating mechanisms for reporting and addressing unethical conduct.
- **Impact:**
- Leaders develop actionable strategies to strengthen ethical practices within their teams, ensuring that ethical leadership is seen as a key component of management at all levels.

As the seminar concludes, Elena gathers all participants for a closing reflection on the day's activities. She reiterates the crucial role that every employee plays in upholding and advocating for ethical standards at OptiTech. She commits to providing ongoing support and resources for ethical decision-making.

Employees leave the seminar with a deeper appreciation for the impact of ethics on organizational behavior and a clearer understanding of how their actions contribute to the ethical stature of OptiTech. They feel empowered and responsible for maintaining high ethical standards in their work.

As the attendees exit, there's a renewed sense of commitment in the air. Conversations center around implementing the insights gained into everyday work practices. Elena watches with satisfaction, confident that the seminar has further solidified the foundations of an ethically driven organizational culture at OptiTech.

Ethical Dilemmas and Decision-Making Frameworks

Building on the momentum from the seminar on the importance of ethics in organizational behavior, Elena decides to deepen OptiTech employees' understanding of ethical decision-making processes by hosting a workshop titled "Resolving Ethical Dilemmas: Frameworks for Decision Making." This event takes place in OptiTech's interactive learning center, equipped with digital polling systems, scenario-based role-playing setups, and private booths for contemplative analysis.

As OptiTech's diverse array of employees—from engineers to sales representatives—enter the learning center, they're greeted by an atmosphere of inquiry and reflection. Each station is designed to engage them in practical exercises that simulate ethical dilemmas they might face in their roles at OptiTech. Elena, aiming to empower her staff with robust tools for ethical decision-making, has organized a series of activities that not only highlight common dilemmas but also teach structured approaches to resolve them.

Elena begins the workshop with a detailed introduction to ethical decision-making, explaining how ethical dilemmas often involve conflicts between values that are important to individuals and the company. She emphasizes the relevance of these situations to OptiTech's daily operations and long-term success, and introduces several key ethical decision-making frameworks that will guide the day's activities.

CHAPTER 13: ETHICS AND CORPORATE SOCIAL RESPONSIBILITY

Interactive Activities:

1. **Framework Tutorials:**

- **Activity:**
- Participants rotate through stations where different ethical decision-making frameworks are explained, such as Utilitarianism, Kantian Ethics, Virtue Ethics, and the Rights Approach. Each station includes practical exercises to apply these frameworks to hypothetical business scenarios.
- **Impact:**
- These tutorials provide participants with multiple lenses through which to view ethical dilemmas, enhancing their ability to analyze and resolve issues from different ethical perspectives.

1. **Role-Playing Ethical Dilemmas:**

- **Activity:**
- In role-playing exercises, employees act out scenarios involving complex ethical dilemmas, such as data privacy breaches, conflicts of interest, and scenarios involving pressure to cut corners on safety for cost savings.
- **Impact:**
- Acting out these dilemmas helps participants practice navigating tricky situations in a controlled environment, where they can discuss and evaluate the outcomes of their decisions with peers and facilitators.

1. **Group Decision-Making Challenges:**

- **Activity:**
- Teams work together to solve complex ethical dilemmas using a structured decision-making framework. They must consider not only the ethical aspects but also the business impacts of their decisions.
- **Impact:**
- Collaborative decision-making exercises reinforce the importance of diversity in perspective and the value of group dialogue in reaching ethical decisions that everyone can support.

1. **Digital Reflection Booths:**

- **Activity:**
- Participants spend time in individual reflection booths where they use an interactive software program to record their thoughts on the ethical frameworks and the decisions they made during role-plays. The software provides feedback and alternative considerations based on ethical theories.
- **Impact:**
- This introspective activity allows employees to reflect on their personal ethical beliefs and the influence these have on their professional decisions, fostering a deeper understanding of their own values and biases.

At the workshop's conclusion, Elena gathers all participants to discuss the day's learnings. She stresses the importance of consistency and fairness in applying ethical principles and how these efforts reflect on OptiTech's reputation and success. She encourages ongoing engagement with ethical training and provides resources for continued learning.

Employees leave the workshop equipped with practical tools and a clearer framework for handling ethical dilemmas in their daily work. They feel more confident in their ability to make well-considered decisions that align with both OptiTech's values and their personal integrity.

As the employees disperse, their thoughtful, engaged discussions suggest a genuine commitment to upholding the ethical standards discussed. Elena watches with pride, reassured that OptiTech is fostering not only a culture of innovation but also one of deep ethical commitment.

Corporate Social Responsibility (CSR) Initiatives

Following a profound workshop on ethical dilemmas and decision-making frameworks, Elena is keen to channel OptiTech's renewed commitment to ethics into tangible actions that benefit society at large. She organizes a comprehensive CSR initiative launch day, titled "OptiTech Cares: Committing to Our Community," held at OptiTech's central campus which is transformed into a vibrant hub featuring interactive booths, partnership announcements with non-profits, and CSR project sign-up stations.

As OptiTech employees from all departments assemble, they are greeted by a festive atmosphere that underscores the company's commitment to giving back to the community. Each booth illustrates different CSR initiatives, ranging from environmental sustainability projects to technology education programs for underprivileged communities. Elena, determined to weave CSR into the very fabric of OptiTech's operations, has designed the day to be both informative and engaging, encouraging every employee to participate actively.

Elena opens the event with an impassioned speech about the role of corporate entities in society and the responsibility OptiTech holds to lead by example. She highlights recent global challenges and stresses the importance of corporate contributions to broader societal solutions. Elena then unveils OptiTech's expanded CSR program, which includes new partnerships and enhanced commitments to sustainable practices.

Interactive Activities:

1. **Environmental Sustainability Pledge:**

- **Activity:**
- Employees are invited to commit to OptiTech's new sustainability goals by signing a large digital pledge board. The goals include reducing carbon footprints, enhancing recycling protocols, and adopting green technologies within office spaces.
- **Impact:**
- This public commitment helps reinforce personal accountability and encourages employees to integrate sustainability into their daily operations and decision-making processes.

1. **Tech for Good Challenges:**

- **Activity:**
- Teams participate in challenges to develop tech-based solutions for non-profit partners. These include creating

educational apps for students in underserved regions or designing software that helps small businesses streamline their operations.
- **Impact:**
- Engaging employees in hands-on problem solving for social causes not only fosters team cohesion but also demonstrates the direct impact of their skills and OptiTech's technology on societal issues.

1. **Volunteer Fair:**

- **Activity:**
- A fair where local charities and community organizations set up booths. Employees explore volunteer opportunities that align with their interests and skills, ranging from mentoring STEM students to participating in community clean-up days.
- **Impact:**
- The fair connects employees with volunteer opportunities, helping them see the direct benefits of their engagement and fostering a deeper connection with the community.

1. **CSR Impact Workshops:**

- **Activity:**
- Workshops led by CSR experts help employees understand how to measure the impact of their CSR initiatives and improve upon them. Topics include effective altruism, impact tracking, and ways to leverage OptiTech's resources for maximum community benefit.

- **Impact:**
- By learning about impact measurement, employees can see the tangible outcomes of their efforts, which boosts morale and motivates continuous participation.

As the day winds down, Elena gathers everyone for a closing ceremony where she thanks them for their enthusiasm and commitment. She discusses the importance of maintaining momentum in CSR initiatives and how these efforts reflect on OptiTech's values and legacy.

Employees leave the event feeling inspired and more connected to OptiTech's social mission. They appreciate the clear linkage between their daily work and its potential to effect positive change in the world.

As the campus slowly empties, the discussions among employees brim with ideas and plans for personal involvement in CSR activities. Elena watches the crowd disperse, feeling a profound sense of pride and optimism, confident that OptiTech is not only advancing technology but also advancing societal well-being.

The Impact of Ethical Conduct on Organizational Success

With OptiTech's CSR initiatives well underway and an engaged workforce, Elena feels the need to reinforce the fundamental importance of ethical conduct in maintaining and enhancing OptiTech's reputation and success. To do this, she organizes a high-profile conference titled "Integrity at the Core: Ethical Conduct and Organizational Success," held at OptiTech's main auditorium, now transformed into a

CHAPTER 13: ETHICS AND CORPORATE SOCIAL RESPONSIBILITY

professional yet inviting environment conducive to serious discussions and reflections on ethics.

As OptiTech's employees, stakeholders, and invited business leaders gather, they are greeted by an atmosphere of solemnity and purpose. The auditorium is lined with panels displaying instances of OptiTech's commitments to ethical practices and their positive impacts on the business. Elena, determined to highlight the tangible benefits of ethical behavior, has arranged for industry experts, ethicists, and top executives from firms known for their ethical standards to share insights and strategies.

Elena begins the conference with a compelling overview of the interplay between ethical conduct and business success. She underscores that integrity should not just be part of the company policy but a cornerstone of OptiTech's identity, crucial for sustaining long-term success and public trust.

Interactive Activities:

1. **Panel Discussions on Ethical Leadership:**

- **Activity:**
- Panels featuring business leaders who have navigated complex ethical dilemmas share their experiences and outcomes. These discussions focus on cases where ethical decisions resulted in positive business outcomes, reinforcing the value of doing the right thing.
- **Impact:**
- These real-world stories provide practical examples of how ethical leadership not only avoids crises but also builds brand loyalty, attracts talent, and enhances investor

confidence.

1. **Workshops on Ethics and Compliance:**

- **Activity:**
- Experts lead workshops on creating robust ethical guidelines and compliance mechanisms within business operations. Participants learn about the latest tools and methodologies for monitoring and enforcing ethical standards.
- **Impact:**
- Equipping employees with knowledge and tools to uphold high ethical standards ensures that OptiTech's operations remain transparent and above reproach.

1. **Ethics in Innovation Labs:**

- **Activity:**
- In these labs, R&D teams discuss and plan how to integrate ethical considerations into the product development process, particularly in areas prone to ethical risks like AI and data privacy.
- **Impact:**
- Focusing on ethics in innovation ensures that OptiTech's products not only lead the market technologically but also set standards in ethical implementation.

1. **Roundtable on Ethical Culture Building:**

- **Activity:**
- A roundtable session engages leaders in discussions

on methods and strategies for cultivating an ethical workplace culture. This includes handling internal reports of unethical behavior and promoting a culture where employees feel safe to voice concerns.
- **Impact:**
- Strengthening the internal culture around ethics empowers employees at all levels to act as guardians of OptiTech's ethical standards, ensuring small issues are addressed before they escalate.

As the conference concludes, Elena reiterates the critical role of ethics in maintaining OptiTech's industry leadership and public image. She calls for ongoing commitment from every employee, highlighting that ethical behavior is everyone's responsibility and is integral to both personal and organizational success.

Attendees leave the conference with a renewed understanding of how deeply ethics are tied to the fabric of OptiTech's success. They feel more committed to upholding these standards in their daily responsibilities.

As the auditorium clears, the energy is one of resolve and determination. Elena watches the departing crowd, confident that the day's discussions have reinforced the foundations of ethical conduct necessary for OptiTech's enduring success. She knows that with this commitment to ethics, OptiTech is well-positioned to navigate the complexities of the modern business world while maintaining its integrity and achieving sustainable growth.

Developing and Implementing Effective Ethics Programs

After reinforcing the crucial role of ethics in OptiTech's operations and long-term success, Elena feels the urgency to operationalize these ethics into concrete programs. To achieve this, she organizes a specialized workshop called "Ethics in Action: From Vision to Reality" at OptiTech's sprawling corporate campus. The space is meticulously arranged into collaborative zones, each equipped with tools for program design, digital feedback systems, and legal advisory stations to ensure compliance.

As OptiTech's key ethics officers, HR leaders, and department heads assemble, they encounter a setup that promotes active development and refinement of ethics programs. Elena, committed to transforming ethical principles into everyday business practices, has planned an intensive day filled with targeted activities that bridge theoretical ethics with practical application.

Elena opens the workshop with an insightful overview of the necessity of ethics programs that not only comply with legal standards but also embody OptiTech's core values. She emphasizes the need for these programs to be dynamic and responsive to the evolving challenges in technology and business landscapes.

Interactive Activities:

1. **Program Design Workshops:**

   - **Activity:**

CHAPTER 13: ETHICS AND CORPORATE SOCIAL RESPONSIBILITY

- Teams work together to draft detailed ethics programs tailored to various aspects of OptiTech's operations, from R&D to sales and marketing. These workshops are facilitated by experts in corporate ethics and compliance.
- **Impact:**
- This hands-on approach helps teams understand the specific ethical considerations of their departments and integrate practical solutions into their day-to-day operations.

1. **Stakeholder Simulation Stations:**

- **Activity:**
- Participants engage in simulations that involve negotiating ethical dilemmas with different stakeholders, including suppliers, customers, and regulatory bodies. These stations use VR technology to enhance realism and immersion.
- **Impact:**
- Simulations provide a deep understanding of the complexities involved in maintaining ethical integrity in real-world scenarios, enhancing decision-making skills under pressure.

1. **Feedback Integration Loops:**

- **Activity:**
- As teams develop their ethics programs, they present their outlines in an open forum where they receive real-time feedback from peers, legal advisors, and ethics experts. This feedback is integrated into the development process

in iterative loops.
- **Impact:**
- This continuous feedback mechanism ensures that the programs are robust, compliant, and aligned with both legal standards and OptiTech's ethical commitments.

1. **Implementation Planning Sessions:**

- **Activity:**
- Teams plan the rollout of their ethics programs, discussing timelines, resource allocation, and key performance indicators to measure the effectiveness of the programs.
- **Impact:**
- Detailed planning helps ensure that the ethics programs are not only well-designed but also effectively implemented and measurable over time.

As the workshop concludes, Elena gathers all participants for a closing session to reflect on the day's work and the path forward. She underscores the importance of commitment from every level of the organization to breathe life into these ethics programs.

Participants leave the workshop with a clear roadmap for developing and implementing robust ethics programs within their teams. They feel empowered and responsible, equipped with the tools and knowledge to drive ethical behavior at OptiTech.

As the participants disperse, their engaged discussions and determined expressions reflect their readiness to advocate for and uphold the new ethics programs. Elena watches them leave, reassured by the strong foundation laid today, confident that these efforts will foster a culture of integrity that permeates every aspect of OptiTech's operations.

Case Studies on Ethics and CSR

Following the successful development and implementation planning of OptiTech's ethics programs, Elena decides to reinforce the learning with real-world applications. She organizes a day-long seminar titled "Ethics in Practice: Case Studies and Lessons Learned," set in OptiTech's main conference facility. The setup includes various breakout rooms, each themed around different industry challenges and ethical dilemmas, equipped with multimedia presentation tools for in-depth case study analysis.

As OptiTech's employees from various sectors—management, engineering, marketing, and customer service—gather, they find themselves amidst an environment designed for critical analysis and interactive learning. Elena, determined to root the theoretical knowledge of ethics and CSR in concrete examples, has arranged for a mix of internal and external experts to present a series of case studies from both OptiTech and other leading companies.

Elena starts the seminar with a compelling speech about the importance of learning from both successes and failures in ethics and CSR. She explains that the selected case studies highlight practical examples of ethical decision-making and CSR strategies that have either significantly benefited the companies involved or served as important lessons due to their shortcomings.

Interactive Activities:

1. **Case Study Presentations:**

- **Activity:**
- Expert presenters introduce case studies that cover a range of topics, such as handling data breaches ethically, navigating supplier relationships responsibly, and implementing sustainable practices that go beyond regulatory requirements.
- **Impact:**
- These presentations provide participants with insights into how companies can effectively manage ethical dilemmas and CSR challenges, highlighting the implications of these decisions on company reputation and success.

1. **Group Analysis Sessions:**

- **Activity:**
- Participants break into small groups to analyze specific case studies, discussing the ethical and CSR strategies employed, the outcomes, and alternative approaches that could have been taken.
- **Impact:**
- These discussions foster critical thinking and problem-solving skills, allowing employees to apply ethical frameworks in analyzing real-world scenarios and to brainstorm innovative CSR solutions.

1. **Panel Discussion on Ethical Leadership:**

CHAPTER 13: ETHICS AND CORPORATE SOCIAL RESPONSIBILITY

- **Activity:**
- A panel of business leaders who have successfully navigated complex ethical landscapes share their experiences and the importance of ethical leadership in maintaining organizational integrity and public trust.
- **Impact:**
- Hearing directly from experienced leaders provides practical leadership insights and inspires participants to prioritize ethical considerations in their decision-making processes.

1. **Ethics and CSR Integration Workshop:**

- **Activity:**
- This workshop focuses on integrating the lessons learned from the case studies into OptiTech's existing policies and practices. Participants work with CSR and ethics officers to refine company strategies and ensure that these are aligned with best practices and lessons from the case studies.
- **Impact:**
- The integration workshop ensures that real-world applications and ethical considerations are embedded into everyday business operations, enhancing the practical impact of OptiTech's ethics and CSR initiatives.

As the seminar concludes, Elena facilitates a final reflection session where participants share their key takeaways and commitments to apply these lessons in their roles. She emphasizes the ongoing nature of ethical and CSR challenges and the need for continual learning and adaptation.

Participants leave the seminar with a deepened understanding of the complexities of ethical conduct and CSR in business. They are equipped with actionable insights and inspired by examples of successful ethical leadership.

As attendees leave the conference facility, their discussions are animated with plans to implement new ideas and strengthen ethical practices in their work areas. Elena watches on, pleased with the engagement and confident that these real-world examples have equipped her team to uphold and champion OptiTech's ethical and social responsibilities more effectively than ever before.

14

Chapter 14: Work-Life Balance

Amidst the high stakes and rapid pace at OptiTech, CEO Elena Myles has noticed a growing concern among her employees about maintaining a healthy work-life balance. Recognizing the critical impact of employee well-being on productivity and innovation, Elena decides to address this directly. She organizes a comprehensive initiative titled "Balancing Act: Fostering Work-Life Harmony at OptiTech." This event is hosted at a serene retreat center, offering a tranquil environment conducive to reflection and learning, far removed from the bustling office.

As OptiTech's employees gather at the retreat, they find themselves in a calm oasis designed to promote relaxation and introspection. The retreat includes workshops, keynote sessions with life coaches, and interactive activities all aimed at providing employees with tools to manage work-life balance effectively.

Elena begins the retreat with an honest acknowledgment of the pressures inherent in the tech industry. She expresses her commitment to ensuring that OptiTech not only excels in innovation but also in supporting its employees' well-being. She outlines the retreat's agenda, which includes practical sessions on time management, stress reduction techniques, and setting professional boundaries.

Interactive Activities:

1. **Workshops on Time Management:**

- **Activity:**
- Experts in productivity lead workshops that teach various time management techniques, including the Pomodoro Technique, effective prioritization, and the use of digital tools to enhance efficiency without causing burnout.
- **Impact:**
- Participants learn to structure their workday more effectively, allowing for clear delineation between work and personal time, thereby reducing the risk of burnout.

1. **Mindfulness and Stress Reduction Sessions:**

- **Activity:**
- Mindfulness coaches conduct sessions on meditation, breathing exercises, and other stress-reduction practices tailored to busy professionals.
- **Impact:**
- Employees gain skills to manage stress in real-time, fostering a more balanced approach to their personal and professional lives.

CHAPTER 14: WORK-LIFE BALANCE

1. **Panel Discussion on Maintaining Boundaries:**

- **Activity:**
- A panel of experienced professionals from various industries shares their strategies for maintaining healthy boundaries between work and home life, even when working remotely.
- **Impact:**
- Hearing from others who have successfully navigated these challenges inspires employees and provides them with practical ideas that can be implemented in their own lives.

1. **Interactive Sessions on Remote Work Best Practices:**

- **Activity:**
- With many employees working remotely, sessions focus on optimizing home office setups, managing distractions, and staying connected with colleagues in a healthy, productive manner.
- **Impact:**
- These sessions help remote employees enhance their work-from-home setups in ways that support both productivity and well-being.

As the retreat concludes, Elena gathers feedback from the participants and discusses plans to incorporate these practices into everyday routines at OptiTech. She emphasizes the importance of ongoing dialogue about work-life balance and announces the introduction of new policies, such as flexible working hours and mental health days.

Employees leave the retreat feeling valued and supported, armed with new tools and perspectives to help them achieve a healthier work-life balance. They appreciate OptiTech's commitment to their well-being, reinforcing their loyalty and motivation.

As the employees depart, their relaxed demeanors and engaged conversations reflect a renewed sense of balance and purpose. Elena watches them leave, satisfied that OptiTech is nurturing an environment where innovation thrives alongside employee well-being, setting a new standard in the tech industry.

Understanding Work-Life Balance and Its Importance

Realizing the necessity to deepen the understanding of work-life balance, Elena decides to follow up the successful retreat with a comprehensive educational session at OptiTech's headquarters. The session, titled "Mastering the Balance: Understanding and Implementing Work-Life Harmony," is designed to educate employees about the physiological and psychological benefits of achieving balance and the potential risks of neglecting it. The headquarters' auditorium is set up with interactive displays, comfortable seating for roundtable discussions, and areas dedicated to mindfulness and relaxation demonstrations.

As OptiTech employees from all levels gather, they are greeted by a soothing environment aimed at reducing stress. The walls are adorned with infographics about stress management and the benefits of work-life balance, and the stage is set for a series of expert talks and interactive discussions.

Elena begins the session with a heartfelt discussion on

why work-life balance is more crucial than ever in the high-demand tech industry. She shares personal anecdotes about the challenges of managing a growing company while maintaining personal health and relationships, emphasizing that sustainable success requires a healthy balance.

Interactive Activities:

1. **Expert Talks on the Science of Stress:**

- **Activity:**
- Leading psychologists and health experts discuss the effects of chronic stress on health, productivity, and mental well-being. They use scientific data to illustrate how proper work-life balance can lead to improved job performance and personal satisfaction.
- **Impact:**
- Understanding the concrete effects of stress and imbalance empowers employees to take their well-being seriously and to utilize company-provided resources for managing stress.

1. **Interactive Workshops on Balance Techniques:**

- **Activity:**
- Workshops are conducted on time management, setting boundaries, and effective delegation techniques. These are complemented by sessions on relaxation techniques such as yoga, meditation, and proper ergonomics at work.
- **Impact:**
- Employees learn practical skills for managing workloads

and stress, which they can apply both in their professional and personal lives to maintain balance.

1. **Panel Discussion on Personal Experiences:**

- **Activity:**
- A diverse panel of employees who have successfully managed to improve their work-life balance share their strategies and the benefits they have experienced. This session includes an open Q&A, encouraging participants to engage and seek advice relevant to their situations.
- **Impact:**
- Hearing from peers provides relatable insights and realistic examples of how to implement balance strategies effectively within the same work environment.

1. **Roundtable Discussions on Policy Improvements:**

- **Activity:**
- Employees are invited to discuss and suggest improvements to current workplace policies that could better support work-life balance. These discussions are facilitated by HR representatives who can take actionable notes and feedback.
- **Impact:**
- This direct input from employees ensures that workplace policies evolve to meet their actual needs, fostering a supportive and flexible work culture.

As the session wraps up, Elena reiterates the company's commitment to supporting its employees in achieving a sustainable work-life balance. She announces the formation of a new internal committee focused on continually reviewing and enhancing work-life balance policies based on employee feedback and changing needs.

Participants leave the session with a deeper understanding of the importance of work-life balance and equipped with new strategies to implement it. They feel supported by OptiTech's proactive approach and are encouraged to prioritize their well-being as much as their professional output.

As employees slowly exit the auditorium, the atmosphere is one of rejuvenation and optimism. They discuss their new insights and the changes they plan to implement in their daily routines. Elena watches, pleased with the positive impact of the session, confident that fostering an environment that values work-life balance will lead to greater employee satisfaction and productivity at OptiTech.

Company Policies that Facilitate Work-Life Balance

Motivated by the positive feedback from the recent educational session on work-life balance, Elena decides it's time to translate the enthusiasm and insights into concrete policies. She organizes a policy development workshop titled "Shaping Balance: Crafting Policies for a Healthier Workplace," hosted in OptiTech's collaborative workspace, redesigned for the day with various stations for policy brainstorming, feedback collection, and expert consultations.

As employees from various departments assemble, the workspace buzzes with a collaborative and innovative spirit. Elena has invited workplace wellness experts and HR consultants to guide the discussions and ensure that the new policies are both effective and feasible. Each station is equipped with tools for drafting policies, providing feedback, and showcasing best practices from other leading companies.

Elena starts the workshop with a strong message about the importance of institutional support in achieving work-life balance. She explains that while individual efforts are crucial, the company's policies play a pivotal role in enabling and sustaining these efforts. She expresses her commitment to ensuring that OptiTech's policies reflect its dedication to employee well-being and productivity.

Interactive Activities:

1. **Flexible Work Arrangements Station:**

- **Activity:**
- Employees discuss and draft proposals for flexible work hours, telecommuting options, and compressed workweeks. They consider various departmental needs and the potential impacts on productivity and collaboration.
- **Impact:**
- Developing flexible work policies helps accommodate personal needs and preferences, which can reduce stress and prevent burnout, thereby increasing job satisfaction and retention.

1. **Paid Time Off (PTO) Enhancements Booth:**

- **Activity:**
- A booth dedicated to reevaluating PTO policies, where employees can suggest improvements such as increased

leave days, "mental health days," and enhanced parental leave. Feedback is collected through digital surveys and live discussions.
- **Impact:**
- By enhancing PTO policies, OptiTech aims to show its commitment to employees' well-being, recognizing that adequate time off is crucial for rejuvenation and long-term productivity.

1. **Health and Wellness Programs Hub:**

- **Activity:**
- This hub focuses on creating or improving health and wellness programs that include fitness benefits, nutritional seminars, mental health resources, and on-site wellness activities.
- **Impact:**
- Investing in comprehensive wellness programs addresses various aspects of employee health, contributing to a healthier workplace environment and reducing healthcare-related costs.

1. **Childcare and Elder Care Solutions Corner:**

- **Activity:**
- Employees brainstorm on initiating or partnering with childcare and elder care facilities to provide support for working parents and caretakers, discussing potential models and subsidies.
- **Impact:**
- Providing support for childcare and elder care can signif-

icantly relieve personal burdens on employees, enabling them to focus more effectively on their work without compromising their family responsibilities.

As the workshop concludes, Elena reviews the proposed policies and assures the team that their feedback and suggestions will be carefully considered and integrated where possible. She schedules follow-up sessions to finalize and implement the policies, emphasizing the dynamic nature of these initiatives—they will evolve as necessary to meet the workforce's changing needs.

Employees leave the workshop feeling empowered and valued, knowing their input directly contributes to policy changes that affect their daily lives. They appreciate OptiTech's proactive approach in creating a supportive and flexible work environment.

As the participants leave the collaborative workspace, their discussions are lively, filled with optimism about the upcoming changes. Elena watches, confident that the new policies will not only enhance work-life balance but also foster a culture of care and respect throughout OptiTech, ensuring its status as a top workplace in the tech industry.

The Role of HR in Promoting Balance

With new work-life balance policies poised for implementation, Elena recognizes the pivotal role Human Resources (HR) must play in promoting and maintaining these initiatives. To empower HR with the tools and authority needed to succeed, she organizes a strategic development session titled "HR as Balance Advocates" at OptiTech's headquarters. The session transforms the HR offices into vibrant hubs of discussion and planning, with breakout rooms dedicated to specific training modules on intervention strategies, employee engagement, and communication.

As OptiTech's HR team assembles, each member is ready to take on their crucial role as champions of the new work-life balance initiatives. The air buzzes with a sense of purpose and commitment, as each breakout room buzzes with activity and strategizing. Elena has brought in external consultants to facilitate the day, ensuring that HR professionals are equipped with the latest knowledge and techniques in managing and promoting workplace well-being.

Elena opens the session with an impassioned speech about the evolving role of HR in modern businesses, especially tech companies that operate at the bleeding edge of innovation and stress. She underscores that HR is not just a support function but a strategic partner in ensuring employee satisfaction and productivity through effective work-life balance policies.

Interactive Activities:

1. **Work-Life Balance Training Workshops:**

- **Activity:**
- HR professionals participate in workshops that train them on identifying signs of work-life imbalance, conducting effective one-on-ones, and offering personalized solutions to employees struggling to maintain balance.
- **Impact:**
- These workshops enhance the ability of HR to act not only as policy enforcers but as supportive counselors

and advisors, helping them guide employees towards healthier work habits.

1. **Policy Communication Strategies Session:**

- **Activity:**
- A session devoted to developing communication strategies that effectively disseminate work-life balance policies and benefits to the workforce, including how to use internal communication tools and public speaking engagements to their fullest.
- **Impact:**
- Effective communication ensures that all employees are aware of the resources available to them, fostering a culture of transparency and support.

1. **Employee Feedback Systems Development:**

- **Activity:**
- HR teams collaborate to design or improve feedback systems that allow employees to voice their concerns and suggestions regarding work-life balance, ensuring these systems are user-friendly and guarantee confidentiality.
- **Impact:**
- A robust feedback system empowers employees to contribute to the continuous improvement of work-life policies and creates a responsive environment that adapts to employee needs.

1. **Mental Health and Well-being Programs:**

- **Activity:**
- The development of specialized programs that focus on mental health, including stress management workshops, wellness apps subscriptions, and on-site mental health days.
- **Impact:**
- Prioritizing mental health within work-life balance initiatives underlines the company's commitment to the overall well-being of its employees, going beyond physical health and productivity.

As the session wraps up, Elena gathers all HR team members to thank them for their dedication and discuss the rollout of these enhanced roles and responsibilities. She reiterates the company's commitment to supporting them in these efforts and the impact their work will have on OptiTech's culture and success.

HR professionals leave the session feeling empowered and valued, equipped with specific tools and strategies to lead the charge in promoting work-life balance. They are inspired to take proactive steps in supporting employees and implementing policies effectively.

As the HR team disperses, their energized discussions and collaborative plans reflect their readiness to embrace their new roles as advocates for balance. Elena watches them leave, confident that with HR leading the way, OptiTech is on the right path to cultivating a truly supportive and balanced workplace.

Impact of Remote and Flexible Work Arrangements

Acknowledging the shifts in the global work environment and OptiTech's ongoing adaptation to these changes, Elena decides to evaluate the long-term impacts of remote and flexible work arrangements instituted during recent shifts in workplace dynamics. To address this crucial aspect, she organizes an all-hands meeting titled "Reimagining Workspaces: The Long-term Impact of Remote and Flexible Work" in OptiTech's largest conference hall, equipped with virtual connection capabilities to include remote team members.

As OptiTech's employees gather both in person and virtually, the conference hall buzzes with a mix of anticipation and curiosity. The setup includes multiple screens displaying real-time data from employee surveys on remote work, panels for virtual attendees, and live polling stations. Elena, committed to making informed decisions about future work policies, has arranged for expert talks on remote work trends, panel discussions with employees who have thrived in remote settings, and interactive Q&A sessions.

Elena begins with an overview of how the workplace has evolved globally and where OptiTech stands in its journey. She acknowledges the mixed responses to remote and flexible work arrangements and expresses her determination to address challenges while highlighting successes. Her speech sets the tone for a constructive dialogue aimed at shaping the future of work at OptiTech.

Interactive Activities:

1. **Expert Panel on Remote Work Trends:**

- **Activity:**
- Leading experts in workplace innovation present current trends and data on the effectiveness of remote and flexible work environments. They discuss how these trends affect productivity, employee satisfaction, and organizational culture.
- **Impact:**
- This provides a foundation of knowledge that helps employees and management understand the broader context of their experiences and the strategic adjustments needed for long-term success.

1. **Employee-Led Panels on Personal Experiences:**

- **Activity:**
- Panels featuring a diverse group of OptiTech employees share their personal stories and testimonials about remote and flexible work, including the benefits and challenges they have encountered.
- **Impact:**
- Hearing from peers helps demystify the practical aspects of remote work and fosters a shared understanding of different needs and preferences within the workforce.

1. **Workshop on Enhancing Remote Work Infrastructure:**

- **Activity:**
- In breakout sessions, employees brainstorm improvements in technology, communication protocols, and resource distribution to better support remote and flexible work setups.
- **Impact:**
- These workshops allow employees to directly contribute to the development of a more robust and supportive remote work infrastructure, ensuring their voices are heard and their needs are met.

1. **Strategy Session for Hybrid Work Models:**

- **Activity:**
- Elena leads a strategy session to discuss potential models of hybrid work that combine the benefits of in-office and remote setups. This session includes drafting possible schedules, office space reconfigurations, and rotation systems.
- **Impact:**
- By collaboratively designing hybrid models, OptiTech can tailor work arrangements that optimize productivity and employee well-being, drawing on the best aspects of both in-person and remote environments.

As the meeting concludes, Elena synthesizes the discussions and feedback, affirming her commitment to implementing a flexible hybrid model that respects employee preferences while maintaining OptiTech's operational efficiency. She outlines next steps, including pilot programs for proposed models and ongoing assessments to ensure they meet the company's goals.

Employees leave the meeting feeling involved and valued in the decision-making process. They appreciate the thoughtful consideration of their feedback and are optimistic about the potential for a more flexible and responsive work environment.

As the conference hall empties, the energy of empowered collaboration lingers. Elena watches the departing employees, reassured by the constructive dialogue and the community's readiness to embrace a future that respects both individual needs and collective goals. This approach, she reflects, is what will continue to drive OptiTech's innovation and success in an ever-evolving global landscape.

Case Studies on Innovative Work-Life Practices

After evaluating the impact of remote and flexible work arrangements, Elena seeks to further inspire her team by showcasing successful examples from around the world. She organizes a day-long symposium titled "Global Innovations in Work-Life Balance," held at OptiTech's auditorium, now transformed into a global virtual conference room. This setup allows for interactive presentations and live links to companies that are pioneers in work-life balance initiatives.

As OptiTech employees fill the auditorium, screens around the room display introductory videos and stats from global companies known for their innovative work-life practices. Elena has arranged for a diverse array of speakers, including CEOs, HR leaders, and employees from these companies, who connect virtually to share their stories and insights. The environment is charged with anticipation, ready to explore how different cultures integrate work-life balance into their corporate ethos.

Elena opens the symposium with a speech about the importance of learning from others and the potential to adapt successful practices to fit OptiTech's unique culture. She emphasizes the global nature of work-life balance challenges and the need for solutions that are both innovative and adaptable.

Interactive Activities:

1. **Case Study Presentations:**

- **Activity:**
- Representatives from companies in Europe, Asia, and the Americas present detailed case studies of their work-life balance programs. These include Denmark's results-oriented work environment, Japan's "Premium Friday" initiative, and Brazil's corporate exercise programs.
- **Impact:**
- These presentations offer a window into how companies across different cultural contexts approach the challenge of balancing work and life, providing practical ideas that can be considered and potentially adapted by OptiTech.

1. **Panel Discussion on Implementation Challenges:**

- **Activity:**
- A panel comprising leaders from companies that have successfully implemented unique work-life strategies discuss the challenges they faced and how they overcame them.

This session includes a live Q&A, allowing OptiTech employees to engage directly with the panelists.
- **Impact:**
- This discussion sheds light on the common hurdles companies face when changing traditional work patterns and how persistent, creative problem-solving can lead to significant improvements in employee satisfaction and productivity.

1. **Workshop on Adapting Global Practices to Local Contexts:**

- **Activity:**
- In facilitated workshops, OptiTech employees work in groups to adapt the presented practices to the specific needs of their teams and projects at OptiTech. They consider factors like local labor laws, corporate culture, and employee demographics.
- **Impact:**
- These workshops encourage employees to think critically about the applicability of global practices within their own work environment, fostering creativity and problem-solving skills.

1. **Innovation Labs for New Work-Life Practices:**

- **Activity:**
- Employees participate in "innovation labs," where they brainstorm and develop new work-life balance initiatives inspired by the day's case studies, guided by expert consultants in organizational psychology and HR management.

- **Impact:**
- These labs serve as incubators for new ideas, potentially leading to groundbreaking work-life balance policies at OptiTech.

As the symposium concludes, Elena summarizes the day's learnings and expresses her enthusiasm for the potential transformations at OptiTech. She commits to supporting pilot projects for the most promising initiatives discussed and encourages a company-wide dialogue to continue exploring these ideas.

Participants leave the symposium energized and inspired, equipped with global perspectives and concrete examples of how work-life balance can be realistically and beneficially integrated into corporate practices.

As employees disperse, their animated discussions reflect a broadened outlook on the possibilities for enhancing their work-life balance at OptiTech. Elena watches with satisfaction, confident that the symposium has planted seeds for innovative practices that could lead to significant, positive changes in how OptiTech supports its employees.

15

Chapter 15: Looking Ahead: The Future of Organizational Behavior

As OptiTech stands at the crossroads of significant growth and technological innovation, CEO Elena Myles recognizes the need to look forward and plan for how these changes will shape the organization's behavior and culture. To envision and strategize for the future, Elena organizes a forward-thinking summit titled "FutureScape: Envisioning Tomorrow's Organizational Behavior" at OptiTech's newly inaugurated Future Center—a space equipped with the latest in digital collaboration technologies, virtual reality setups for simulating future work environments, and an amphitheater for large-scale discussions and presentations.

OptiTech's leaders, key employees, and invited futurists gather in the Future Center, buzzing with anticipation and curiosity. The center is a hive of activity, with various zones dedicated to exploring trends in technology, workforce dynamics, and global business practices. Elena has designed the summit to not only predict future trends but also to actively shape them, ensuring OptiTech remains at the forefront of the industry.

Elena opens the summit with an inspiring speech about the dynamic nature of organizational behavior and the forces reshaping it—technological advancements, globalization, and changing employee expectations. She challenges everyone to think beyond current practices and to imagine the possibilities that lie ahead.

Interactive Activities:

1. **Trend Analysis Workshops:**

- **Activity:**
- In these workshops, futurists and organizational behavior experts present emerging trends and their potential impacts on workplace dynamics, such as AI in leadership, the rise of remote global teams, and the integration of gig workers into traditional business models.
- **Impact:**
- Participants gain insights into future trends and start to conceptualize how these could be harnessed to enhance OptiTech's operational and strategic goals.

1. **VR Simulations of Future Workplaces:**

- **Activity:**
- Participants use virtual reality to experience simulations of future work environments, including highly automated offices, virtual global meetings, and digital nomad hubs.

- **Impact:**
- These immersive experiences provide a tangible sense of future work settings, helping participants to visualize and plan for changes in organizational structure and employee interactions.

1. **Scenario Planning Sessions:**

- **Activity:**
- Teams engage in scenario planning exercises to develop strategies for potential future challenges, such as managing a fully remote workforce, integrating advanced AI into decision-making processes, and maintaining corporate culture in a highly diverse and globalized team.
- **Impact:**
- By preparing for various future scenarios, OptiTech ensures its resilience and adaptability, whatever the future holds.

1. **Innovation Labs for Organizational Practices:**

- **Activity:**
- Innovation labs focus on designing new organizational practices that align with anticipated changes in the business environment. These include new models of employee engagement, performance management systems, and leadership development programs tailored for a future where human and AI collaboration is the norm.
- **Impact:**
- These labs allow OptiTech to stay ahead of the curve, developing practices that not only respond to future

trends but also actively shape them.

As the summit wraps up, Elena emphasizes the importance of ongoing innovation in organizational behavior and the need for continuous learning and adaptation. She announces the creation of a new Future Insights Team at OptiTech, dedicated to continuously tracking and responding to emerging trends.

Participants leave the summit energized and inspired, equipped with a broader perspective on the future of work and organizational behavior. They are committed to being proactive rather than reactive, playing an active role in shaping the future of OptiTech and the industry.

As the attendees disperse, filled with new ideas and a sense of purpose, Elena reflects on the productive discussions and innovative concepts that emerged. She feels confident that with these preparations and the collective talent of her team, OptiTech is well-positioned to lead, adapt, and thrive in the ever-evolving landscape of organizational behavior.

Emerging Trends in Organizational Behavior

Building on the momentum of the "FutureScape: Envisioning Tomorrow's Organizational Behavior" summit, Elena plans a targeted workshop to delve deeper into specific emerging trends that are poised to reshape the landscape of organizational behavior at OptiTech. The workshop, titled "New Frontiers: Embracing Emerging Trends in Organizational Behavior," is held in OptiTech's innovation lab, a space designed to foster creativity and forward-thinking, equipped with interactive tech displays and collaborative brainstorming areas.

As OptiTech's leaders and key innovators gather, they find themselves surrounded by stations showcasing cutting-edge technologies and methodologies, including data-driven behavioral analytics, AI-enhanced HR tools, and virtual collaboration platforms. Elena has organized a series of expert-led sessions and hands-on demonstrations to explore these trends thoroughly and to strategize their integration into OptiTech's practices.

Elena opens the workshop with a dynamic presentation on the rapid evolution of organizational behavior influenced by advancements in technology, changes in global workforce demographics, and a shift towards more dynamic, team-based structures. She highlights specific trends such as remote work technologies, the gig economy, and the rise of corporate social responsibility, emphasizing the opportunities they present for OptiTech.

Interactive Activities:

1. **Behavioral Analytics Demonstration:**

- **Activity:**
- A live demonstration of behavioral analytics tools that use big data to predict employee behavior patterns, identify potential HR issues before they escalate, and tailor management practices to individual team dynamics.
- **Impact:**
- This allows leaders to see firsthand how leveraging data can improve decision-making and help tailor leadership styles to better meet the needs of their teams.

1. **Workshop on Integrating Gig Workers:**

- **Activity:**
- An interactive workshop addressing the challenges and strategies for integrating gig workers into traditional teams, focusing on maintaining cultural coherence and ensuring compliance with labor regulations.
- **Impact:**
- Participants develop actionable plans for harnessing the flexibility of the gig economy while maintaining organizational standards and employee satisfaction.

1. **Roundtable on Remote Work Innovations:**

- **Activity:**
- A roundtable discussion featuring remote work experts who share the latest innovations in virtual collaboration tools and strategies for maintaining productivity and engagement in a dispersed workforce.
- **Impact:**
- This discussion offers insights into optimizing remote work arrangements to benefit both the company and employees, emphasizing the balance of flexibility and productivity.

1. **CSR Initiative Brainstorming Session:**

- **Activity:**
- Teams brainstorm new CSR initiatives that align with OptiTech's business objectives and values, focusing on sustainability, community engagement, and ethical gov-

ernance.
- **Impact:**
- By aligning CSR efforts with business strategies, OptiTech reinforces its commitment to ethical practices and community responsibility, enhancing its corporate image and employee morale.

As the workshop concludes, Elena synthesizes the discussions into a strategic roadmap for integrating these emerging trends into OptiTech's operational fabric. She emphasizes the importance of agility and continuous learning, committing to regular updates and adaptations as these trends evolve.

Participants leave the workshop inspired and equipped with a clearer understanding of how to proactively incorporate these emerging trends into their strategies and daily operations. They feel prepared to lead OptiTech through the evolving landscape of organizational behavior with confidence and innovation.

As attendees leave the innovation lab, their conversations buzz with ideas and plans for immediate action. Elena watches with satisfaction, assured that OptiTech is not just responding to changes in organizational behavior but is actively shaping them, staying ahead of industry curves and setting standards for the future.

The Impact of Globalization on Organizational Practices

Recognizing the profound influence of globalization on business operations, Elena convenes a strategic forum titled "Global Reach: Navigating the Waves of Globalization" at OptiTech's main campus. The forum is designed to foster a deeper understanding of globalization's challenges and opportunities, equipped with global communication links for real-time interaction with OptiTech's international teams and expert guest speakers from around the world.

As OptiTech's senior leaders, managers, and key stakeholders gather in the forum, they find themselves surrounded by digital displays showing real-time data and trends from global markets. The space is organized to facilitate open discussions, workshops, and live case studies focusing on the nuances of global operations. Elena aims to equip her team with strategies to leverage globalization for competitive advantage, emphasizing cultural sensitivity, regulatory compliance, and operational efficiency.

Elena opens the forum with an insightful presentation on the current global landscape, highlighting the rapid changes in international trade, cross-cultural workforce dynamics, and technological advancements. She stresses the importance of understanding these trends to effectively navigate and succeed in a global marketplace.

Interactive Activities:

1. **Global Market Trends Workshop:**

- **Activity:**
- Experts in global market analysis lead a workshop where participants analyze emerging trends in key markets where OptiTech operates. The focus is on understanding regional differences in consumer behavior, regulatory environments, and technological adoption.
- **Impact:**
- This workshop helps leaders appreciate the complexity of global markets and tailor OptiTech's strategies to fit diverse consumer and regulatory landscapes.

1. **Cross-Cultural Management Training:**

- **Activity:**
- A series of training sessions on cross-cultural management, including communication styles, negotiation techniques, and leadership in diverse cultural settings. These sessions are facilitated by cultural experts and supported by real-life case studies from OptiTech's international teams.
- **Impact:**
- Training enhances managers' skills in leading diverse teams, crucial for maintaining employee engagement and productivity across OptiTech's global operations.

1. **Roundtable on Global Compliance:**

- **Activity:**
- Roundtable discussions focus on navigating complex global regulatory frameworks. Legal experts and compliance officers provide insights and strategies to ensure that OptiTech's operations adhere to international laws and standards.
- **Impact:**
- These discussions provide critical knowledge needed to manage risks associated with global operations, safeguarding OptiTech against legal and ethical violations.

1. **Innovation Labs for Global Collaboration:**

- **Activity:**
- Innovation labs challenge participants to create solutions that enhance collaboration across OptiTech's international offices. This includes developing new communication tools, virtual team-building activities, and collaborative platforms tailored to the needs of a global workforce.
- **Impact:**
- By fostering innovation in global collaboration tools and practices, OptiTech strengthens its internal connections, ensuring cohesive and aligned global operations.

As the forum concludes, Elena emphasizes the interconnected nature of today's business world and OptiTech's role within it. She underscores the importance of agility and adaptability in global practices and pledges continuous support for initiatives that enhance global integration.

Participants leave the forum equipped with deeper insights and practical strategies for optimizing OptiTech's global operations. They feel better prepared to lead their teams in a world where understanding and leveraging globalization is key to organizational success.

As the attendees disperse, their animated discussions reflect a renewed commitment to embracing global challenges as opportunities. Elena watches, reassured that OptiTech is moving forward with a clear and informed strategy, ready to make a mark on the global stage while respecting and adapting to local contexts.

The Evolving Nature of Work and Worker Expectations

After successfully navigating discussions on globalization, Elena identifies another pressing trend: the rapidly changing nature of work and evolving worker expectations. To address this, she organizes a visionary conference titled "The Future of Work: Evolving Expectations and Practices," hosted in OptiTech's innovative space, which is transformed into a future-focused think tank. This setup includes interactive tech displays, areas for brainstorming, and stages for panel discussions featuring diverse voices from within and outside OptiTech.

As employees from various departments and levels gather, they're greeted by a dynamic environment that reflects the cutting edge of workplace technology and design. Elena has invited futurists, workforce researchers, and young innovators to share their insights, ensuring a comprehensive exploration of current trends and future possibilities.

Elena starts the conference with a thought-provoking overview of how technology, generational shifts, and global connectivity are reshaping what workers expect from their employers and their careers. She emphasizes the need for OptiTech to proactively adapt its practices to meet these changing expectations and to continue attracting and retaining top talent.

Interactive Activities:

1. **Panel Discussion on Generational Shifts:**

- **Activity:**
- A diverse panel including Gen Z innovators, Millennial leaders, and experienced Gen X and Baby Boomer professionals discuss their distinct workplace expectations, focusing on flexibility, purpose-driven work, and technology use.
- **Impact:**
- This discussion illuminates the varied needs and motivations across different age groups, helping OptiTech understand how to cater to a multi-generational workforce effectively.

1. **Workshops on Flexible Working Models:**

- **Activity:**
- Participants engage in workshops to design flexible work models that accommodate remote work, freelance options, and compressed hours, reflecting the increasing demand for work-life integration.
- **Impact:**
- These models aim to enhance employee satisfaction and

productivity by offering choices that align with modern lifestyles and work preferences.

1. **Innovation Labs for Employee Engagement:**

- **Activity:**
- Innovation labs focus on using technology to boost employee engagement. These include developing apps for better workplace communication, virtual reality setups for remote collaboration, and AI tools for personalized career development paths.
- **Impact:**
- By integrating these technologies, OptiTech aims to lead in creating an engaging, inclusive, and flexible working environment that responds to the needs of today's and tomorrow's workers.

1. **Roundtable on Ethics and Transparency:**

- **Activity:**
- A roundtable on the importance of ethics, transparency, and corporate responsibility in meeting worker expectations. Discussions cover data privacy, fair treatment, and the ethical use of AI in the workplace.
- **Impact:**
- Strengthening these areas ensures that OptiTech remains a trusted and appealing employer, critical for attracting and retaining a workforce that values integrity and openness.

As the conference wraps up, Elena reflects on the insights

gained and the strategies discussed. She commits to taking concrete steps to implement these ideas, starting with pilot projects for the flexible work models and the deployment of new engagement tools. She underscores the ongoing commitment required to adapt to these evolving expectations and to foster an innovative and responsive workplace culture.

Participants leave the conference energized and inspired, equipped with a deeper understanding of the evolving nature of work and the strategic adaptations necessary for OptiTech to remain competitive and desirable as an employer.

As attendees leave, their conversations buzz with ideas and enthusiasm for the future. Elena watches on, proud of the proactive discussions and the collective commitment to adapt and thrive amidst the evolving workplace landscape, confident that OptiTech is well-prepared to meet the future with innovative practices and an empowered workforce.

Future Challenges of Organizational Leaders

After a series of insightful conferences and workshops aimed at navigating the complexities of the evolving workplace, Elena turns her attention to the specific challenges that future leaders at OptiTech will face. To tackle this crucial topic, she organizes a leadership retreat titled "Leading Into Tomorrow: Navigating Future Challenges," hosted at a serene lakeside resort designed to facilitate deep thinking and strategic planning away from the daily hustle of corporate life.

OptiTech's current and up-and-coming leaders gather in a setting that combines natural beauty with high-tech facilities, designed to inspire innovative thinking and foresighted strategies. The retreat includes guided sessions on scenario

CHAPTER 15: LOOKING AHEAD: THE FUTURE OF ORGANIZATIONAL...

planning, ethical leadership, and adapting to technological advancements, with expert facilitators from various fields.

Elena opens the retreat with a reflective speech on the responsibilities of leadership in an ever-changing corporate world. She emphasizes the critical roles that foresight, adaptability, and ethical integrity will play in shaping the future of OptiTech. She outlines the sessions designed to prepare OptiTech's leaders to meet these challenges with confidence and competence.

Interactive Activities:

1. **Scenario Planning Workshops:**

- **Activity:**
- Leaders participate in scenario planning workshops that present hypothetical future situations ranging from economic downturns to breakthrough technological innovations. Each scenario challenges leaders to devise strategic responses that ensure company resilience and growth.
- **Impact:**
- These exercises sharpen the leaders' strategic thinking skills and their ability to anticipate and react to various potential futures, ensuring that OptiTech can navigate any eventuality.

1. **Ethics and Leadership Roundtables:**

- **Activity:**
- Roundtable discussions focus on the ethical dilemmas

that leaders may face, including those involving AI and data privacy, global workforce management, and sustainability challenges. Ethics experts facilitate these discussions to guide leaders in forming principled decision-making frameworks.
- **Impact:**
- These discussions reinforce the importance of maintaining a strong ethical foundation in all decision-making processes, which is crucial for building trust and integrity in leadership roles.

1. **Digital Transformation Sessions:**

- **Activity:**
- Interactive sessions led by tech innovators explore the implications of new technologies on business operations and workforce management. Leaders learn about the latest tools and strategies for integrating AI, machine learning, and blockchain into their business practices.
- **Impact:**
- Leaders gain firsthand knowledge of cutting-edge technologies and learn how to effectively implement these tools to optimize performance and innovation at OptiTech.

1. **Communication and Influence Workshops:**

- **Activity:**
- Expert communicators conduct workshops on effective communication strategies, focusing on influencing and motivating a diverse, global, and sometimes remote

workforce.
- **Impact:**
- Leaders enhance their communication skills, ensuring they can effectively convey vision, drive change, and inspire their teams across all levels of the organization.

As the retreat concludes, Elena gathers feedback and reflections from the participants, discussing how the insights gained can be integrated into their leadership practices. She reiterates her commitment to supporting their growth with continuous training and leadership development opportunities.

Leaders leave the retreat equipped with new skills, insights, and strategies to face the future challenges of leading a dynamic and rapidly evolving company like OptiTech. They feel empowered and ready to implement what they've learned, confident in their ability to guide their teams toward continued success.

As the leaders depart from the tranquil retreat setting, their determined strides and thoughtful expressions reflect a readiness to tackle the future, whatever it may hold. Elena watches them, proud of their growth and confident in their ability to steer OptiTech through the uncertainties of the future with wisdom, vision, and integrity.

The Role of Sustainability in Organizational Behavior

After successfully addressing the challenges future leaders will face, Elena shifts her focus to a pivotal aspect that is reshaping the global business landscape: sustainability. Recognizing its profound influence on organizational behavior and corporate identity, she organizes a landmark event titled "Green Future: Integrating Sustainability into Organizational Behavior" at OptiTech's eco-friendly conference center, designed with sustainable materials and powered by renewable energy.

OptiTech's key stakeholders, project leaders, and environmental consultants converge at the conference center, a testament to OptiTech's commitment to sustainability. The center is a beacon of green technology, with systems displaying real-time energy savings and waste reduction statistics. Elena plans to dive deep into how sustainability can be woven into every aspect of organizational behavior, from daily operations to long-term strategic planning.

Elena begins with a compelling speech on the urgent need for sustainability in today's business practices, not just as a response to environmental challenges but as a core element of OptiTech's operational ethos. She underscores the importance of sustainability in driving innovation, attracting talent, and building a lasting brand that customers and employees trust and support.

Interactive Activities:

1. **Sustainability Workshops:**

- **Activity:**
- Facilitated by leading environmental experts, these workshops cover essential topics such as carbon footprint reduction, sustainable supply chain management, and green product innovation.
- **Impact:**
- Participants learn specific strategies to reduce environ-

mental impact and develop new business practices that promote ecological sustainability while driving economic growth.

1. **Panel Discussion on Sustainable Leadership:**

- **Activity:**
- A panel featuring CEOs from leading sustainable companies shares insights on integrating eco-friendly practices into corporate leadership and decision-making.
- **Impact:**
- These discussions inspire and educate OptiTech's leaders on the benefits of sustainable leadership, emphasizing the role of executive commitment in achieving significant environmental goals.

1. **Green Tech Innovation Challenge:**

- **Activity:**
- OptiTech employees from various departments participate in a challenge to devise innovative solutions that leverage technology to enhance sustainability, such as energy-efficient computing or biodegradable electronics components.
- **Impact:**
- This challenge not only stimulates creativity but also aligns technological innovation with sustainability goals, fostering a culture of green innovation at OptiTech.

1. **Sustainability Reporting and Metrics Seminar:**

- **Activity:**
- Experts in sustainability metrics conduct a seminar on the importance of transparent and accurate reporting of sustainability efforts, including how to track and communicate progress to stakeholders.
- **Impact:**
- This seminar equips participants with the knowledge to measure and report on sustainability effectively, ensuring accountability and continuous improvement.

As the event concludes, Elena reflects on the discussions and initiatives proposed throughout the day. She commits to integrating the suggestions into OptiTech's strategic plans and announces the formation of a new Sustainability Task Force to oversee these initiatives. She emphasizes that sustainability is an ongoing journey that requires consistent effort and innovation.

Employees leave the event with a renewed understanding of the critical role sustainability plays in modern organizational behavior. They are motivated to contribute to sustainability efforts, knowing their actions have a direct impact on the company's environmental footprint and social responsibility.

As attendees leave the conference center, there's a sense of collective purpose and determination in the air. Their discussions are filled with ideas and plans to implement sustainable practices in their roles. Elena watches them depart, confident that OptiTech is on the right path to becoming a leader in sustainable business practices, setting a standard for the industry and creating a legacy that extends beyond technology and into environmental stewardship.

Preparing for the Future Workplace

In the wake of successful discussions about sustainability and innovation at OptiTech, CEO Elena Myles turns her focus towards preparing the entire organization for the rapid changes that define the future workplace. Recognizing the need for a company-wide initiative, she organizes a pioneering event titled "Future-Proofing OptiTech: Strategies for a Changing World," held at OptiTech's main auditorium, now transformed into a futuristic hub with immersive tech demonstrations and interactive strategy stations.

OptiTech's employees, from entry-level to senior management, gather in a venue designed to inspire and engage. Interactive displays around the room showcase emerging technologies like augmented reality workspaces and AI-driven analytics tools, illustrating their potential impact on daily work routines. Elena has scheduled a full day of activities, including keynote presentations by futurists, skill-building workshops, and panel discussions with industry leaders who have successfully navigated significant workplace transformations.

Elena opens the event with a visionary speech about the evolution of the workplace driven by technological advancements, demographic shifts, and changing global economic landscapes. She emphasizes the importance of agility, continuous learning, and adaptability, outlining how OptiTech must evolve its practices to stay competitive and maintain its industry leadership.

Interactive Activities:

1. **Keynote Presentations on Technological Advancements:**

   - **Activity:**
   - Futurists and technologists give presentations on the latest advancements in artificial intelligence, machine learning, and blockchain, discussing their potential to transform current business models and workflows.
   - **Impact:**
   - These presentations help employees understand the scope of technological changes and stimulate thinking about how their roles might evolve in response.

1. **Workshops on New Skill Development:**

   - **Activity:**
   - Interactive workshops focus on building new skills that are likely to be in high demand, such as data literacy, digital collaboration, and cyber-security awareness.
   - **Impact:**
   - By enhancing their skill sets, employees are better prepared to tackle new challenges, contributing to both personal career growth and the company's success in a future digital landscape.

1. **Panel Discussions on Adaptive Leadership:**

   - **Activity:**
   - Seasoned leaders from various industries share insights

into managing teams through periods of significant change, emphasizing the importance of adaptive leadership and resilience.
- **Impact:**
- Listening to experienced leaders provides practical strategies for OptiTech's managers to lead effectively, fostering a culture of adaptability and proactive change management.

1. **Scenario Planning Sessions:**

- **Activity:**
- Teams participate in scenario planning exercises to anticipate potential future challenges and brainstorm responses. These scenarios range from dealing with a digital-first marketplace to managing a global crisis.
- **Impact:**
- Scenario planning strengthens strategic thinking and preparedness, enabling OptiTech to remain agile and responsive no matter what the future holds.

As the event draws to a close, Elena gathers all participants to consolidate the day's learnings and commitments. She emphasizes the collective responsibility to drive OptiTech forward and adapts to the fast-evolving corporate world. Elena announces the establishment of a Future Readiness Task Force, dedicated to implementing the strategies devised during the event and ensuring that OptiTech continues to innovate and lead.

Employees leave the event invigorated, with a clear understanding of the evolving workplace and their roles within it.

They are motivated by the new tools and knowledge acquired, ready to apply these insights to their daily responsibilities and long-term career plans.

As attendees disperse, their lively discussions reflect a renewed commitment to innovation and adaptability. Elena watches with pride, confident that OptiTech is well-prepared to embrace the future, equipped with a workforce that is not only ready to meet upcoming challenges but to thrive amidst them.

About the Author

Goodson Mumba is a multifaceted individual known for his diverse expertise and prolific contributions across various fields. As an infopreneur, thought leader, and spiritual leader, he has inspired countless individuals through his insightful teachings and impactful writings. Mumba is also an accomplished author, with several notable works to his name, including "Understanding Corporate Worship," "The Years I Spent in a Week," "Management By Harmony," "The CEO's Diary," "Change to Change" and "Creative Thinking for results" His literary works span topics ranging from business management to personal development and spirituality, reflecting his broad range of interests and insights.

With a Master of Business Leadership (MBL) and a Bachelor of Arts in Theology (BTh), Mumba brings a unique blend of business acumen and spiritual wisdom to his work. His educational background is further enriched by a Group Diploma in Management Studies, providing him with a solid foundation in organizational dynamics and leadership principles. Additionally, Mumba holds diplomas in Education

Psychology, Leadership and Management Styles, Organizational Behaviour, Financial Accounting, Economic Growth and Development, and Project Management, showcasing his commitment to continuous learning and professional development.

Mumba's expertise extends beyond traditional academic disciplines, encompassing areas such as Neuro-Linguistic Programming (NLP) and Positive Psychology. His diverse skill set is complemented by a range of certifications, including Creative Problem Solving and Decision Making, Life Coaching Fundamentals and Techniques, Professional Life Coaching, and Performance Management System Design. These certifications reflect Mumba's dedication to equipping himself with the tools and knowledge necessary to empower others and drive positive change.

As an author, Mumba's writings reflect his deep understanding of human nature, organizational dynamics, and spiritual principles. His works offer practical insights, actionable strategies, and inspirational guidance for individuals seeking personal growth, professional success, and spiritual fulfillment. Mumba's holistic approach to life and leadership resonates with readers worldwide, making him a respected figure in both the business and spiritual communities.

Overall, Goodson Mumba's diverse background, extensive knowledge, and profound insights make him a sought-after speaker, mentor, and author. His commitment to excellence, lifelong learning, and service to others continues to inspire individuals to unlock their full potential and lead lives of purpose and significance.

Goodson Mumba is renowned for initiating the concept of Management by Harmony, revolutionizing traditional management practices with a focus on balanced and holistic approaches. He has authored two influential books on this subject: "Introduction to Management by Harmony" and its sequel, "Management by Harmony."

Mumba's work has significantly impacted the field, offering innovative strategies for fostering organizational harmony and efficiency. His contributions continue to shape contemporary management theories and practices.

www.ingramcontent.com/pod-product-compliance
Lightning Source LLC
Chambersburg PA
CBHW071825210526
45479CB00001B/4